BEHIND THE GARDEN WALL

Behind the garden wall

A History of Capital Punishment in Belfast

by

STEVEN MOORE

GREYSTONE

1995

For my wife Heather and children
Nicholas, Andrew and Christopher

First published 1995

Greystone Books Ltd., Caulside Drive, Antrim, Northern Ireland

ISBN 1 870157 26 5

Designed by Rodney Milller Associates, Belfast.

Printed by W&G Baird Ltd., Antrim.

FOREWORD

MANY people have helped in the preparation of this book. Friends, colleagues and in some cases complete strangers have gone out of their way to offer assistance in the search for information or photographs. To each I offer my sincere thanks.

The staff at the Central Library, and particularly its Newspaper Library, have been exceedingly patient and helpful. Likewise, the librarians at the Linenhall Library and the Bangor Branch Library, the latter doing all they could to supply what must have seemed like an endless list of requested books. I also spent many fascinating hours at the Public Record Office of Northern Ireland, and thank the staff there.

Thanks must go to former Belfast High Sheriff Jim Walker and Robin Boyd at the City Hall for permission and assistance respectively to go through the council files, and to the Presbyterian Church for access to its collection of the Witness newspaper.

There are several individuals connected with the Prison Service who it would be imprudent to name but without whose help the task would have been immeasurably more difficult and less rewarding.

I owe a special debt of gratitude to Mike McComb, head librarian at Century Newspapers, who allowed me free access to the bound News Letter volumes in his care and kindly gave permission for a number of photographs to be reproduced. Also his assistant Vicky Weir, who helped with the illustrations.

Many of the illustrations have been supplied by the Ulster Museum, the National Library of Ireland and the Public Record Office. In addition, can I thank the Rev Frank Donnelly, parish priest of St Peter's Church, Drogheda, for the photograph taken by himself of the head of Oliver Plunkett, and the National Graves Association for a picture of hanged IRA man Tom Williams. My brother-in-law William Stockdale, who gave freely of his time and considerable photographic skills to supply many of the illustrations, deserves particular credit.

Last, but not least, I must thank my wife Heather who, in addition to proof-reading, has listened without complaint for the past three years to me talking endlessly about this or that aspect of hanging.

It is almost inevitable that inaccuracies slip into a work of this nature. For those, I alone take responsibility.

Steven Moore

RECORD OF EXECUTIONS

Henry Joy McCracken (and others)	Cornmarket	June/July 1798	Rebels
John Doe John Magill	Castle Place	6 September, 1816	Weavers
Robert O'Neill	Belfast Prison	21 June, 1854	Soldier
Daniel Ward	Belfast Prison	8 April, 1863	Carpenter
John Daly	Belfast Prison	26 April, 1876	Coal porter
Arthur McKeown	Belfast Prison	14 January, 1889	Car driver
John Gilmore	Belfast Prison	17 August, 1894	Farmer
William Woods	Belfast Prison	11 January, 1901	Dealer
Richard Justin	Belfast Prison	19 August, 1909	Labourer
Simon McGeown	Belfast Prison	17 August, 1922	Labourer
Michael Pratley	Belfast Prison	8 May, 1924	Tailor
William Smiley	Belfast Prison	8 August, 1928	Farm labourer
Samuel Cushnan	Belfast Prison	8 April, 1930	Farm labourer
Thomas Dornan	Belfast Prison	31 July, 1931	Farmer
Eddie Cullens	Belfast Prison	13 January 1932	Cinema worker
Harold Courtney	Belfast Prison	7 April, 1933	Lorry driver
Thomas Williams	Belfast Prison	2 September, 1942	Labourer
Samuel McLaughlin	Belfast Prison	25 July, 1961	Foundry worker
Robert McGladdery	Belfast Prison	20 December, 1961	Labourer

CONTENTS

BEHIND THE GARDEN WALL

*Which is more immoral; which is
more inhuman? For the State legally
and deliberately to execute a
convicted murderer or to see
further innocent lives being
taken because the murderer is
spared the supreme penalty?*

Lord Dunleath

(Capital punishment debate, December, 1974)

Twenty-five years of terrorist violence has left
Crumlin Road Jail surrounded by extensive
security fencing (News Letter).

BEHIND the garden wall, deep within the grounds of Her Majesty's Prison Belfast, popularly known as Crumlin Road Jail, lie the remains of the 17 men who paid the ultimate price for their crimes. It has been more than 30 years since the last body was lowered into the earth there, concealed within its plain softwood coffin, and placed in an unmarked grave. There is no longer any garden behind the wall, the vegetable plots having given way to a tarmac carpark for prison staff. A gravel road runs round the jail, within a few feet of the graves. There is even the possibility it crosses over some where it passes through the gateway in the wall.

Today the jail is primarily used as a remand centre, though a small number of sentenced prisoners are housed there to carry out the day-to-day routine tasks. It is doubtful if any of the present inmates, some perhaps facing murder charges, would have cause to reflect on those before them who paid the supreme penalty for their crimes.

Capital punishment came comparatively late to Belfast. Indeed, it took a revolution, in 1798, to precipitate the first executions. After the County Courthouse and County Jail were built opposite each other on the Crumlin Road in the middle of the 19th century, Belfast succeeded Carrickfergus as the centre for State killings in County Antrim.

Carrickfergus acquired its county jail in the second half of the 18th century, appropriately on Antrim Street, next door to the courthouse which today serves as the Town Hall. That jail was demolished towards the end of the last century, and an ordnance depot put up in its place. Today the site is occupied by a shopping complex and historical visitor centre that tells the story of old Carrick.

Her Majesty's Prison, Belfast has greatly changed since the last executions were carried out in 1961. This picture shows the circle area from which the four wings radiate (Prison Service).

The change of county town came with Belfast's rapid growth during the 19th century. By the time building work began on the county jail and courthouse in Belfast, the town's population was rapidly heading towards the 90,000 mark. At the turn of the century it had grown to almost 350,000.

As might be expected, housing, sanitation and other facilities and amenities failed to keep pace with the growth in demand and much of Belfast consisted of hovels where morality and respect for law and order were of scant regard. Crime escalated rapidly and for most of the 19th century the county assizes were dominated by business from Belfast, leading to the creation of a "County of the City of Belfast Assizes" specifically to deal with it.

The first execution at the Crumlin Road jail was in 1854, the last in 1961. Because the legal system operated on a county basis during most of this period, the majority of those executed came from County Antrim. Later, the creation of Northern Ireland at partition led to a radical shake-up in the judicial system, with the Crumlin Road gallows playing host for the first time to killers from further afield.

The ground floor of Crumlin Road Jail's C Wing
today. It was at the end of this wing that the
scaffold was permanently housed from the turn of
the century (Prison Service).

All those executed within the precincts of Belfast jail were convicted murderers and
all were from working class backgrounds. There were labourers and farmers, a soldier, an
IRA terrorist, an American Jew, an alcoholic tramp, a lorry driver and a car driver, this last
of the horse-drawn variety.

Several of the killings revolved around unmarried girls becoming pregnant or giving
birth, and the shame which that involved in less enlightened times. Sex, in a much more
ugly form, was also the motive in other murders, while robbery, jealousy and resentment
borne of bullying would account for most of the rest.

In many instances the guilt of the hanged man appeared unquestionable and was often
supported by an admission on the eve of execution. A few cases are not so clear cut,
however. One in particular leaves the distinct impression that a man may have been
executed for a murder the jury thought he intended to commit, had his alleged victim not
died by accident.

SECTION ONE

A PLACE IN HISTORY

CHAPTER ONE

A BRUTAL PAST

Boys, you need not be in such a hurry;
there can be no fun till I come.

(Victim of the Carrick gallows)

Sir Arthur
Chichester, who
played a
prominent role in
the Elizabethan
conquest of Ulster,
was granted a patent to
develop the lands around
Belfast Castle
(Linenhall Library).

THE TAKING of a life in retribution for an injustice long pre-dated the arrival of the Normans in Ireland, an event which imported a system of laws from outside the island. Before the birth of Christ, the ancient Britons were throwing their enemies into pits or on to sinking sand to die and hanging is known to have been practised by the Anglo-Saxons, though other, often more crude, methods were common.

The Normans, however, were different in that they virtually put a halt to the executing of prisoners, with the exception of those found guilty of conspiring against the Crown. Nine hundred years later, in 1965, the House of Commons did the same. In between, thousands upon thousands of people suffered the humiliation and excrutiating pain of the hangman's rope, the vast majority of them victims of severe laws which condemned even petty criminals to the gallows.

The reintroduction of capital punishment in a general form dates from around the time of the succession to the English throne of King John in 1199. A Royal Charter, issued following the monarch's visit to Ireland in 1210, extended the Common Law of England to the parts of Ireland under English control.

Elsewhere in Ireland, of course, Gaelic law survived, and nowhere more so than in Ulster. Under native law, the killing of another person was considered a civil rather than a criminal offence, which could be made good by paying compensation. There were exceptions, such as the hanging of a man at Derry in 1197 for stealing from a church, though that was probably as much in response to a public outcry over the sacrilegious nature of the crime as anything else. Those found guilty of killing respected members of the community, and those who couldn't pay the compensation demanded, also faced the death sentence, often being burnt alive.

In turn, Irish custom resulted in a watering down of the Common Law imported from England, with the death penalty for murder often downgraded to a fine. Indeed, by the end of the 13th century this had become normal practice and very few people, least of all those of English descent, actually ended up on the gallows but instead were handed out fixed penalties.

The last province to see the full introduction of English Common Law was Ulster, which remained the most Gaelic part of Ireland until the final bloody Elizabethan conquest. By 1603 the Irish champion Hugh O'Neill had been defeated and in the same year Sir Arthur Chichester, who had ruthlessly and effectively applied Mountjoy's scorched earth policy, was rewarded with the grant of a patent for the lands around Belfast Castle - the first major step in the development of the city.

A few years before, in June 1597, the military garrison at Belfast Castle had been attacked by the Clandeboye O'Neills and "all the English men in the ward were hanged and their throats cut, and their bowells cutt oute of their bellyes." (Jonathan Bardon, Belfast: An Illustrated History).

The English victors quickly saw to it that the court system applying in the rest of Ireland, including execution, was introduced to Ulster. The most famous Irish 17th century victim of the gallows, however, was not hanged in Ireland but at that most notorious site of gruesome ritual, Tyburn in London.

It was in December, 1679 that Oliver Plunkett, Archbishop of Armagh, was arrested and imprisoned in Dublin Castle on a charge of high treason. Taken to London to stand trial, he was found guilty on the false evidence of two Franciscan monks and sentenced to be hanged, drawn and quartered. He was

The head of Oliver Plunkett, cut from the body during the ritual dismemberment which followed his execution at Tyburn, was smuggled away to Rome. It eventually returned to Ireland and is now permanently housed in St Peter's Church, Drogheda (Fr Frank Donnelly).

taken to Tyburn on 1st July, 1681, where that most infamous of executioners, Jack Ketch, half strangled him by allowing the cleric to swing from the noose for several minutes. Then he was cut down so his heart and entrails could be cut from his body and burnt on the scaffold fire. The corpse was finally beheaded and cut into four pieces.

The archbishop's remains, however, were not to rest in peace. The severed head was secretly removed from the scaffold during the bloody ritual of dismemberment and later turned up in Rome. In 1722 it was returned to Ireland and eventually placed in St Peter's Church, Drogheda, Co Louth. The rest of the body was buried in the cemetery of St Giles in the Fields church in central London, but not before the arms had been amputated below the elbows as religious relics. The coffin was later exhumed and moved to a

Benedictine abbey in Germany before being returned to England and St Gregory's Monastery, Bath, towards the end of the 19th century.

Almost 20 years earlier at Tyburn, in 1662, another name well remembered in Irish history, Oliver Cromwell, was also to join the list of those hanged on its gallows - despite already being dead. The Roundhead who brought so much terror to Ireland was taken from his tomb in Westminister Abbey on the orders of Charles II, who desperately wanted revenge for his father's execution. Cromwell's body, plus the bodies of his son-in-law Henry Ireton and John Bradshaw, who had also taken part in the trial and sentencing of Charles I, were allowed to hang from the Tyburn gallows most of the day before being cut down, their heads chopped off, placed on pikes, and displayed at Westminster Hall.

Such was the popularity of the rope as a means of meting out justice that an average of 2,000 people a year were being hanged in England alone during the reign of Henry VIII, with only marginally fewer under Elizabeth I. Likewise in Ireland, the gallows on Dublin's St Stephen's Green were seldom idle, providing regular entertainment for vast crowds of the lower classes who flocked to watch the spectacle. Belfast at that time was still in the shadow of Carrickfergus, a little further along the lough shore. Holding the principle position in the county, Carrick was well able to provide the required facilities when it came to exercising the full rigours of the law. For many years its scaffold, situated on Gallows Green, was known as the Three Sisters. Its three stone columns, three feet in diameter and 18 feet high, were connected by wooden beams which allowed three criminals to be hanged at a time. In Robert Young's volume, Ulster in '98, John Coates, a one-time secretary to the Antrim Grand Jury, recalled vividly both the procedure and some of its victims:

> The modus operandi was as follows: On leaving the gaol, the cart, of the old two-solid-wheel kind, with the coffin crossways on it, went first, with the hangman; then the condemned walked behind, and on each side a file of soldiers, fully armed. When the cart was drawn under the fatal beam, the prisoner stood on it with the clergyman, who prayed with him till the hangman put the noose over his head, pulled the cap down on his face, and gave the signal to withdraw the cart.
>
> At one execution a man was suspended so low that his foot touched the ground. A soldier stepped forward and caught up the limb, so as to let him choke comfortably. He was ever after called the 'Hangman'.
>
> On one occasion the boys were rushing along the hedges so as to get near the scaffold for a good view, when the criminal shouted to them, 'Boys, you need not be in such a hurry; there can be no fun till I come'.

The Three Sisters were later dismantled and executions transferred to the County Jail in the town centre.

Oliver Cromwell, whose Roundhead army took
Belfast in an assault on the North Gate in 1649,
ended up on the scaffold after his death as
Charles II desperately tried to avenge his father's
execution. Illustration by John Carey
(Linenhall Library).

By the beginning of the 18th century there were some 50 offences punishable by
death, a vast increase on medieval Common Law which deemed that only the most
serious of crimes, including murder, treason, arson and rape, qualified as capital offences.
The industrial revolution in England, with its emphasis on material wealth and property,
led to a huge increase in lawlessness and a corresponding rise in harsh laws. As towns and
cities mushroomed, so did the instances of prostitution, child labour, drunkenness and
extreme poverty on one hand, and the activities of pickpockets, thieves and highwaymen
on the other. Parliament, pressed to take action, passed statutes by the dozen which were
intended to stem the tide of criminality.

Over the next hundred years there came into being what was known as the Bloody
Code, with more than 220 pieces of legislation which contained provisions for capital
sentences. Each of these was capable of being interpreted so as to apply to a multitude of
offences. For example, the notorious Waltham Black Act, enacted by Parliament in
response to a spate of poaching in Hampshire, was eventually invoked to create more than
350 capital offences, ranging from carrying an arm to having a blackened face, taking a

The Three Sisters scaffold, at Gallows Green on
the outskirts of Carrickfergus, could despatch up
to three victims at a time (Linenhall Library).

fish, cutting down a cherry tree, stealing turnips or writing threatening letters. Likewise
the Larceny Law, passed to clamp down on burglary, was interpreted to cover the theft of
anything over 12 pence in value.

The fault lay largely with the Common Law system itself, which left it to the judges
to determine the scope of vaguely worded Acts. Consequently, if one judge accepted that
a certain offence fell within the bounds of a particular Act, other judges followed suit, and
so the list of capital crimes grew.

An unsavoury aspect of judgments at this time was the stipulation of mutilations and
other cruelties as part of the sentence. The most popular of these, particularly for those
accused of treason, was to have the victim hanged, drawn and quartered. This involved
stringing them up by the neck, perhaps for 10 minutes, so they suffered the pain of the
rope without succumbing to strangulation. After being cut down, and while still alive, the
executioner set about them with a knife, severing the genitals, cutting out the intestines
and heart and burning them before the crowd. Finally the head was severed and the body
cut into four quarters for display on some public place.

Fortunately, such ritual barbarity on the scaffold was gradually phased out, though
even as late as 1789 the Belfast News Letter was still reporting:

> *The following persons were tried and found guilty at the assizes of Clonmel:*
> *Edmond Duggan, otherwise Crosskeen, for poisoning Catherine Gueray, to*
> *be hanged, quartered, and beheaded on Saturday the 28th instant. Alice*
> *Daniel, otherwise, Duggan his wife, for the life offence, to be strangled and*
> *burned to ashes the same day, James Keane, for a burglary, committed at*
> *Golden-bridge, to be hanged the same day. Philip Murray, for horse stealing,*
> *to be hanged on the 4th of April next.*

Members of the Royal Irish Constabulary, with
presumably one of the sergeant's daughters, pose
for the camera around 1890. The RIC took over
from the Belfast force after the latter was accused
of being sectarian in its handling of the 1864 riots
(Public Record Office).

Women were not subjected to the punishment of being hanged, drawn and quartered, for fear it would offend the spectators. Instead, they were usually burnt at the stake. The Alice Daniel mentioned above was one of the last to suffer this form of execution, which was repealed by Parliament the following year. A Bill passed in 1814 stipulated that drawing and quartering should be carried out only after the prisoner's death by hanging.

Newspaper reports at the end of the 18th century show just how common the death sentence was. At the Down Assizes in March, 1789, for example, Patrick Campbell was found guilty of picking the pocket of James Smyth in Newry of £1 14s 8d and sentenced to be hanged on 9th May; at Omagh in April Thomas Hughes was found guilty of a double murder near Ballygawley which had already seen members of two families, the O'Donnellys and McGoughs, executed the previous year. Several months later Miles

Donnelly was similarly condemned to be hanged and beheaded for the same killing; also in April, and at the same court, John McAfee was sentenced to be hanged for house-breaking, Pat Nugent for rape and David Hog for robbery; in May, Dan Doughterty was condemned to die at Londonderry Assizes for breaking into a house near Claudy with his face blackened, while Charles Stewart, caught with his hand in the pocket of some unfortunate on the stairs of the courthouse on the Saturday of the same assizes, was also sentenced to be hanged; in August, Edward Armstrong was found guilty of murdering his infant son and executed several days later. His wife had died suddenly shortly before and in court Armstrong had blamed his impoverished state for the killing.

Interestingly, a woman sentenced to death for robbery in October, 1789, was reprieved after claiming she was pregnant. A jury, consisting of 13 women stopped at random in the street, was formed to determine whether or not she was telling the truth. Fortunately for her, they found in favour of the "wretched looking creature, without shoe or stocking".

The tide was turning, however, with the 50 years preceding 1860 seeing the vast majority of statutes covering capital punishment being repealed. The following year, 1861, the Criminal Law Consolidation Act was passed. It reduced the number of capital crimes to just four: murder, treason, arson in docklands and piracy. There were two reasons for this aboutturn: first a campaign by a dedicated group of Members of Parliament to reform the system and secondly, and perhaps most importantly since it created the security to allow change, the foundation by Sir Robert Peel of the modern police force in England in 1829. As far as policing was concerned, Ireland was in fact well ahead compared to England. As Chief Secretary of Ireland, Peel had created the Peace Preservation Force in 1814, though Dublin and a few other baronies had already their own forces as early as 1778. The 1836 reorganisation of the Irish Constabulary, formed some 14 years earlier, saw the absorption of the PPF and a variety of other units into the national police force, though Dublin, Belfast and Londonderry continued to have their own constabularies.

In 1800, the Irish Parliament, as one of its last actions before being abolished, had passed the Belfast Police Act. The new force was to have a short and chequered history. It was heavily involved in putting down the riots in the town in 1832, 1857 and 1864. Following the last of these, a commission of inquiry produced a damning report of the way in which the police handled the disturbances. The report found that the Belfast force had only a handful of Roman Catholics in its 160-strong ranks. In June, 1865, its duties were taken over by the Royal Irish Constabulary.

In due course there were further refinements of the legal system. Public executions were abolished in 1868; the hanging of under-16s officially ended in 1908, though no one under 18 years of age had been executed in the previous 20 years; and mothers who killed their babies and pregnant women were excluded from the death penalty in 1922 and 1931 respectively.

The last executions to take place in Britain were in 1964 when two men were hanged at the same time on the same day but in different prisons.

Belfast, *August* 18.

On Saturday laft, Edward Armftrong was execued at Downpatrick, purfuant to his fentence, for the unnatural murder of his own Infant. This unhappy cafe was rendered ftill more deplorable by the circumftance of his Wife having died very fuddenly and unexpectedly not long before. He declared that poverty was the caufe.

James Watfon Hull, Efq; High Sheriff of the county of Down, has been pleafed to appoint Mr. Robert Garrett of Lifburn to be his Under Sheriff, in the place of Mr. Robert Stewart, who, from bad health, has refigned; and Mr. Garrett was in confequence on Wednefday the 12th inft. fworn into office, before the Hon. Baron Hamilton at Downpatrick.

Belfast, *August* 21.

At the late Affizes for the county of Antrim, held at Carrickfergus, which ended on Monday laft, Jofeph Blackwood of Belfaft, butcher, charged with the murder of George Emerfon on his return from Hillfborough Races—was acquitted. In confequence of an Appeal, by the next of kin, a new trial will be held in the Court of King's Bench, Dublin, on next Michaelmas term, which commences on the 3d day of November next.

At the fame Affizes, Hugh Giffen was found guilty on one indictment of ftealing three fheep; and on a fecond, for ftealing a firkin of butter, &c.—to be tranfported.

Edward Robinfon and John Knox were indicted for being loofe idle vagrants and vagabonds—to be tranfported purfuant to the ftatutes, unlefs they give fecurity within fix months to be of the peace and keep good behaviour.

James Orr the elder and James Orr the younger, found guilty of ftealing from Mrs. Margaret Henry, at Ballymoney, one quarter of a hundred of potatoes, value fixpence, to be privately whipped, imprifoned one week, and to remain in jail until they fhall give fecurity before two magiftrates to be of the peace for three years.

The sentence of death was regularly passed by Ulster courts in the 18th century, though not all those who found themselves in the dock on capital charges ended up on the gallows. From the Belfast News Letter, 1789.

CHAPTER TWO

THE FIRST TO DIE

*I am just going to do my last duty
to my country. It can be done as well
on the scaffold as on the field.*

Rebel leader Robert Emmet

(Executed September 1803)

The Battle of Antrim, at which Henry Joy
McCracken led his rebel forces in an unsuccessful
bid to take the town. The illustration,
by J W Carey, was drawn almost 100 years after
the event (Linenhall Library)

Execution of Henry Joy McCracken
and other United Irishmen
June-July, 1798

THE SAVAGERY which followed the rebellion of 1798 far exceeded the blood-letting of the actual battles. The fighting had been marked by confusion, disorganisation and disappointment for the rebels, whose initial gains were quickly lost to the King's forces. Many of the insurgents took to the hills or open countryside in a bid to escape capture, while others returned to their homes in the hope that their part in the uprising would be overlooked or not realised.

Although the main confrontations in the North had been confined to comparatively small areas of counties Antrim and Down, the retribution which followed spread far and wide.

Belfast, which had been under martial law prior to the hostilities for fear it would be a key player in the rebellion everyone knew was threatening, remained calm. The town's rebels, realising the strength of the garrison stationed there, had largely left days previously to join their comrades. Nonetheless, the 1798 rebellion was to produce the first State executions in Belfast.

It is not possible to say with absolute accuracy just how many died on the Belfast gallows that year, though it is known that at least six men were executed during and immediately after the battles.

Shortly after 2am on 7th June, 1798, the first shots of the uprising were fired in a brief and inconclusive confrontation between troops and rebels in Larne, Co Antrim. Within days reports were circulating of uprisings across the county. Rebels had attacked and taken Randalstown and Ballymena, and had only narrowly failed in their attempt to overpower the garrison at Antrim. On 9th June, the County Down insurgents struck at Saintfield.

Undoubtedly feelings were running high in Belfast as news of the uprising spread, accompanied, it may well be assumed, by outlandish rumour. It was in such a climate that William Magill was to meet his fate on Saturday, 9th June. Unfortunately little is known about the man who was to be the first person executed in the town in an orgy of retribution. He was tried, before a court martial, on a charge of "swearing soldiers from their allegiance". His failure to recruit them to the United Irishmen's cause cost him his life. So eager were the soldiers to have him despatched, and so teach the citizens of the town a lesson, that they didn't wait for a scaffold to be erected. Instead, a rope was attached to a lamp-post outside the Market House, on the corner of Cornmarket and High Street, and Magill sent to meet his Maker from the end of it.

As the rebellion crumbled, the troops set about the task of rounding up the ringleaders. Soon a prison ship was moored offshore in Belfast Lough, while the town's army barracks, in Barrack Street, and the Donegall Arms Hotel, in what is today Castle Place, were used to house prisoners brought in from the outlying areas.

A young attorney named James Dickey, from Crumlin, was next to feel the noose about his neck. Found "sulking in a bog" close to Divis Mountain by a party of soldiers, he was brought into Belfast on 25th June, 1798 to stand trial.

The following day he was hauled in front of a court martial sitting in the Exchange Rooms (what today is the Northern Bank on the corner of Waring Street and North Street) and accused of rebellion and treason, to which he pleaded not guilty. Apparently unconcerned at the situation he found himself in, Dickey assured the court he would give them no trouble but would happily acknowledge the truth of any evidence given and contradict what he considered lies. In fact, he offered little defence and even failed to produce witnesses on his behalf despite the court agreeing to a delay to allow him to do so.

During the trial it was alleged that Dickey had been seen on horseback, sword in hand, urging on the rebels. He was said to have used the sword to behead William Crawford, despite the latter begging for mercy, and accused of advocating the putting to death of prisoners captured at the Battle of Randalstown.

The court martial was held over three days, and had to be adjourned several times. On the last day proceedings were suspended for several hours after Dickey turned up insensible, either through alcohol or, as was suspected, after having taken poison. He was revived sufficiently to be found guilty and sentenced to be hanged and his head cut off and placed on top of the Market House. General Nugent, military commander of the Northern District, declined to reverse the court's decision.

At about 8pm that evening, Thursday, 28th June, 1798, Dickey – dressed in a light-coloured coat and grey pantaloons – was brought to the place of execution, in front of the Market House, where he spent almost an hour talking and praying with the Rev Sinclair Kelburn. His whole attitude to his predicament, the Belfast News Letter reported, was "seeming indifference". It went on:

> *About nine o'clock, he mounted a temporary scaffolding, erected at the Market-house, when he asked for a drink of water, which having got, he requested his body would be given to his friends; the executioner then attempted to cover his face with a handkerchief, which prisoner would not allow and in a few moments after he was launched into eternity. After hanging some time, he was taken down and his head severed from his body, which the executioner holding up in his hand exclaimed "This is the head of a traitor". It was then affixed to a spike, and placed on the Market-house.*

Henry Joy McCracken who, despite being the
Northern leader of the uprising, was spared the
beheading of his corpse normally dealt out to
traitors (Ulster Museum).

Dickey's head was not to remain alone atop the Market House for long. The following day the trial of John Storey, who had worked as a printer on the United Irishman's newspaper, The Northern Star, got under way. Storey, from Islandbawn, Muckamore, had been captured in a quarry close to his home. Several witnesses testified to having seen Storey taking an active part in the Battle of Antrim (which he undoubtedly had). Although the court was adjourned until the next morning, so that Storey's father could give evidence in his son's defence, he was subsequently found guilty of rebellion and treason. Again General Nugent declined to exercise his powers of mercy.

Shortly after 2pm on Saturday, 30th June, Storey was brought to the Market House where he was attended by another clergyman, the Rev Baistow. About 3.30pm, he climbed the steps of the scaffold to meet his fate. After hanging for 15 minutes, the body was taken down. The head was cut off and a spike thrust into it so it could be placed in an adjacent corner to Dickey's.

A few days later, on 5th July, it was the turn of Hugh Grimes to face the court martial. He was accused of being a rebel leader at Creevy Rocks, where the County Down insurgents had amassed, and at the battle of Ballynahinch. Brought to the scaffold at 3pm, he spent an hour in devotion with the Rev Dobbs before being executed. After hanging for three-quarters of an hour, he was cut down and the body handed over to his friends for burial.

On the same day that Grimes was tried, another man, Lambert Brice, was sentenced to be executed at Dundonald for being a leader at Ballynahinch and for housebreaking.

The Rev Dobbs also comforted the next man to face the Belfast scaffold. Henry Byers, described as a very young man, was convicted of taking cattle from Mr Price's farm at Saintfield and driving them to the rebel camp at Ballynahinch. He was obviously familiar with the Price household, having recently married the daughter of a servant there. Possibly because of his youth, the court left it to Mr Price to decide whether he should be hanged or not. Price is reputed to have clapped the young man on the back, pointed to the gallows and the heads on spikes beyond, and told him (according to the Rev Thomas Ledlie Birch of Saintfield) to "go boldly for he should soon have plenty of his neighbours for company". Byers, after spending some time with the Rev Dodds, was duly executed on Monday, 11th July, 1798 and his head placed with the others on top of the Market House.

The best remembered citizen to mount the steps of a Belfast gallows, however, was Henry Joy McCracken. The Northern leader of the uprising, McCracken could have been in no doubt as he dressed in his green uniform to take on the Crown forces just what failure would mean. Imprisoned in Dublin's Kilmainham Jail for most of the previous year, he had seen other men pay the extreme penalty of the law for their political beliefs. He wrote to his sister, Mary Ann McCracken, on 9th June, 1797:

> The day before yesterday, we saw from our windows two militiamen conducted to the park by all the military in this neighbourhood, and there shot for being United Irishmen.

Amid scenes of confusion about the scaffold,
erected outside the Market House in High Street,
Henry Joy McCracken mounted the steps and
within seconds was dangling from the hangman's
rope. This illustration is by John Carey and was
drawn almost a century after the execution
(Linenhall Library).

McCracken had been one of those who had secretly left Belfast to meet up with his men at Roughfort, near Doagh. Defeated at Antrim, he spent the next month trying to evade capture, including periods on Slemish and Divis mountains. On 7th July he was arrested near Carrickfergus as he attempted to make his way to a boat which would have taken him to safety. After a spell in the town's jail, he was transferred to Belfast. The following day, Tuesday, 17th July, 1798 he was tried, found guilty, and condemned to die.

Arm in arm, McCracken and his sister walked to the old Market House. Kissing Mary Ann three times, he sent her away with a friend, watching as she disappeared through the crowds. McCracken then attempted to deliver an address, but couldn't be heard above the general commotion and calmly accepted his fate.

Troops, many on horseback, held back the mob as it attempted to surge forward, considerable confusion ensued and within a few minutes McCracken was swinging from the end of the rope.

A boy in the crowd, John Smith, later recalled:

> *Hoarse orders were given by the officers, the troops moved about, the people murmured, a horrible confusion ensued, and in a minute or so the manly, handsome figure on which the impression of nobility was stamped, was dangling at a rope's end. The body was soon cut down, and the only favour extended to it was freedom from mutilation.*

He may indeed have been cut down again in a comparatively short time, though the Belfast News Letter reported the body hung for an hour. The corpse was not beheaded after execution but returned to the family for burial - leading to a desperate but intriguing attempt to revive him in his Rosemary Lane home. His sister had summoned two doctors to come to the house and they immediately began working on the body. Mary Ann recalled years later:

> *From the moment I parted with Harry, the idea which had occurred to me in the morning that it might be possible to restore animation, took full possession of my mind, and that hope buoyed up my strength and supported me at the moment of parting with him. Every effort that art could devise was made, and at one time hopes of success were entertained, but the favourable symptoms disappeared, and the attempt was at length given up.*

McCracken's body was buried in the grounds of what today is St George's Church in High Street. Some years later, the Rev Edward May, brother-in-law of Lord Donegall, tore up the gravestones and sold off the land. In 1902, during demolition work at the corner of Ann Street and Church Lane, what were believed to be the bones of Henry Joy McCracken were uncovered. Seven years later, the remains were reburied in Clifton Street cemetery next to his sister's grave.

Another rebel said to have been hanged at Belfast was George Dickson, who had worked in Dickey's legal practice. Dickson apparently earned the unusual nickname of General Halt after disarming and taking prisoner five soldiers single-handedly by holding a blunderbuss to a sergeant's head, and instructing him to order his troops to lay down their weapons. His prisoners on that day were said to have been among the crowd which watched his execution.

The United Irishmen's cause didn't end in 1798. Another act of rebellion was attempted five years later, in July 1803, by Robert Emmet in Dublin. He was hanged two months later. The Northern leader of that rebellion was Thomas Russell, the "man from God-knows-where". Despite evading capture initially, Russell was eventually taken prisoner in Dublin and transported to Downpatrick, where he was hanged outside the gateway of the County Down Jail on 21st October, 1803.

High Street in 1791, with the Market House on
the right. It was here, on a temporary scaffold,
that the United Irishmen were executed
(Ulster Museum).

FOOTNOTE: The bid to revive Henry Joy McCracken was not entirely a forlorn
hope. There are several instances recorded where a hanged person was later found
to be alive. In 1651, a woman named Ann Greene was executed, and the body left
hanging for almost half-an-hour. Cut down and placed in a coffin, she began to
show signs of life. A startled soldier, perhaps as an act of mercy, clubbed her with the
butt of his musket. Later, as a surgeon was about to begin dissection, a small rattling
sound came from her throat. She was bled and placed in a warm bed. A month later,
Ann was well enough to return to her family. She died nine years later, having
married and borne three children since her "execution".

Another woman who survived hanging was Margaret Dickson in 1728. She was
cut down after approximately an hour. Her family, taking the body for burial,
stopped at an inn for refreshments on the way home. While there, a noise was heard
coming from the coffin. The lid was lifted and Margaret sat up - causing panic
among staff and customers! She survived another 25 years and had several children.

Executions of John Doe and John Magill
6th September, 1816

SHORTLY after four o'clock on a cold winter's morning, a terrific explosion ripped through the home of Francis Johnston, a muslin manufacturer, who lived in a fine house at the top end of North Street, near Peter's Hill in Belfast. An armed gang, eight to 10 strong, then rushed the front door and began firing wildly into the blackness, with the blunderbuss of Mr Johnston being the only response from inside. The commotion had raised the neighbours from their slumbers and the night watchmen, who had only passed the house a short time earlier, were already on their way back. Faced with the prospect of capture, the gang disappeared into the night.

It was, in fact, the second attack on Mr Johnston's home in seven months. Both incidents stemmed from the severe hardships being endured by Belfast weavers, many of whom were then either without work or struggling on meagre wages. In 1811 the industry, which two years before had hit a low, was booming again as the Napoleonic wars effectively eliminated foreign competition. The good times could not last forever, however, and prices began to fall again, with finished cloth only fetching two-thirds of its previous value by 1816. Even during the better times a weaver's life had been difficult, with earnings often less than 15 shillings a week out of which had to come money to pay for an assistant and materials, and sometimes the rental of a loom stand.

While some were fortunate enough to be employed by factories, the vast majority worked from hovels in the poorer areas of the town. As they were on piece work, (that is being paid for what they actually produced) the fall in price really stung.

Although it was against the law, the weavers formed unions, or combinations as they were known, in a bid to try to force employers to take a more responsible attitude to wages. Johnston, it would appear, was particularly despised and the union tried to stop weavers working for him altogether.

But on 28th February, 1816, a group of weavers went too far. In what was obviously a well planned operation, the gang arrived outside the Johnston household in the early hours of the morning. Inside were sleeping the master and mistress of the house, their eight children, two maids and a manservant. The weavers began by prising off the shutters on the parlour window and pulled aside the iron bars put there to frustrate just such an attack. Raising the sash, they threw in a box filled with pitch, tar and hemp to which they had attached a ball of gunpowder - a sort of early fire bomb-cum-blast bomb. The fuse was lit and the gang retreated across the road to await the blast.

In the meantime, however, the manservant had been awakened by their efforts to break in. He came down the stairs armed with a pitchfork, with which he stabbed the bomb and carried it through the house to the kitchen door. Then he rushed upstairs again to waken his master who, armed with a fully loaded blunderbuss he kept by his bed, took up position at a front room window. From there he opened fire on the gang sheltering on the far side of the street. Seconds later the bomb exploded, blowing out the windows and doors but - deprived of its pitch, tar and hemp - doing comparatively little damage.

The weavers, perhaps unaware of how little they had achieved, then rushed forward firing, with Johnston replying in kind. The fracas ended within a few seconds with no-one on either side injured.

Nonetheless, what was being described as an "atrocious outrage" could not go unpunished and five men were arrested and brought before the County Assizes in Carrickfergus that August. Three, John Doe, John Magill and Joseph Madden were accused of burglary at the Johnston home, and the other two, James Dickson and James Park, of conspiracy in the affair. All were found guilty, with Doe, Magill and Madden, despite a plea for mercy from the jury, sentenced to be hanged on 6th September, 1816. Dickson and Park were given 18 month jail terms, ordered to be publicly whipped, and bound over to keep the peace for what was a huge sum in those days of £100, with two sureties of £50 each. Both the executions and the whippings were to be carried out in Belfast, ruled the judge, as an example to others of a like mind in the town.

The hangmen, however, were to be denied one of their fees. Shortly before the day of execution, the Lord Lieutenant accepted the jury's plea and changed Madden's sentence to transportation for life. So it was that at nine o'clock the following Friday morning only two prisoners were brought through the doors of Carrick jail to join the procession

DREADFUL OUTRAGE.

£2000 REWARD.

WHEREAS, on WEDNESDAY morning the 28th February, instant, about FOUR o'Clock, an Armed Party attacked the Dwelling-House of Mr. FRANCIS JOHNSON, in Peter's-hill, in the Town of Belfast, and after breaking the Windows, introduced some extremely combustible preparation, which exploded with such violence, as to destroy a great part of the said House and imminently endangered the lives of the whole family, (consisting of Thirteen Persons).

Now we, whose Names are hereunto annexed, viewing with indignation and horror, this infamous and malicious attempt to involve in destruction not only the Property of this respectable Gentleman and the lives of himself and Family, but those of all the neighbourhood, and anxious to bring to Condign Punishment the Perpetrators of this atrocious and diabolical outrage, do hereby promise to pay, in proportion to the sums to our names annexed, a REWARD of

TWO THOUSAND POUNDS Sterling,

to any Person or Persons, who shall, within Twelve Months from this date, discover on, and prosecute to conviction the Person or Persons, or any of them, concerned in this atrocious outrage; and we also hereby engage to pay a REWARD of

FIVE HUNDRED POUNDS,

for such Private Information as may lead to the discovery and conviction of any Person or Persons who were concerned aiding or assisting therein, and the name of the Person or Persons who shall make such private communication will be kept secret.

Application will also be made to Government for obtaining his Majesty's most gracious Pardon for any Person or Persons implicated in the above outrage, who shall give such information as may lead to conviction.

Belfast, 28th February, 1816.

The eminent citizens of Belfast were so outraged at the attack on Francis Johnson's home that they put up a reward of £2,000, a huge sum in its day, for information leading to a successful prosecution of the culprits, and another £500 for the capture of those who may have helped them (Belfast Commercial Chronicle).

Castle Place in 1843. It was on the widest part of
the road, close to the Donegal Arms, seen on the
right of the picture, that the scaffold was erected
for the executions of John Doe and John Magill
(Ulster Museum).

forming up outside for the trip to Belfast. Doe and Magill were put in a chaise (a light
open carriage), into which also squeezed two of the three clergymen in attendance. This
allowed the huge crowd of spectators which gathered outside the jail and along the route
to catch a final glimpse of the condemned men. Behind followed two carts, the first
carrying the county executioner and part of his apparatus. Another executioner "from a
distant county" sat in the second cart, his face covered in black crepe to disguise his
identity. A strong military detachment, consisting of the 5th Dragoon Guards and several
companies of the Royal Scotch, formed up front and rear of the procession. At a slow and
solemn pace, the convoy set off.

By noon the prisoners were nearing the town, and their imminent arrival was signalled
by a large detachment of troops, both on horse and foot, leaving the Belfast barracks and
taking up position along the upper end of High Street to Castle Place, where the
procession came to a halt.

While the prisoners sat in the chaise engaged in religious devotions with the
clergymen, a temporary gallows was erected. It consisted of two triangles and a cross beam,
the whole about 15ft high. When it was complete, Doe and Magill were led out of the
carriage and on to the platform, which was the second of the carts from Carrick.

Further devotions took place, with the prisoners praying fervently. Doe then read several passages from the New Testament "with a strong and audible voice" before giving his dying declaration, part of which read:

> As I am shortly to stand before the judgment seat of Jesus Christ, the following, in the presence of God my Saviour, are my last words, dying declaration, and true confession: I was formerly a professor of the Gospel, and united to a Church of Christ, but, forgetful of my profession, I fell from the truth, cohabited with a woman of bad character, was cut off from the Church, and thus, from step to step, was brought under the awful deserved chastenings of the Lord. I acknowledge, that although I have not been guilty of all the crimes laid to my charge on my trial, yet I have transgressed the laws of my country, and do justly merit the execution of the sentence announced upon me.

Magill declined to deliver his own declaration, but handed a paper to one of the clergymen to read. In it he denied some of the charges against him, in particular denouncing the evidence of "the approver Gray" and his wife that he had asked Gray to a meeting of muslin weavers in Mill Street. He did admit, however, his guilt on the main charge:

> I confess, however, with the deepest contrition, that I was present when the outrage was committed on Mr Johnston's house. I now see and am extremely sorry that I acted under the influence of mistaken views. I was taught to believe that Mr Johnston's family did not sleep in their own house. I had no idea of taking any lives. I now see the evil of all such combinations and outrages, though I once thought them innocent and even laudable.

With the speeches finished, the clergymen climbed down from the platform. The two executioners completed their work, placing the caps over the men's faces and tightening the nooses about their necks. Stepping down, they went to the front and quickly led away the horse and cart, leaving the men dangling. Doe, it was said, scarcely moved, while Magill had "strong convulsions" for several minutes before he too stopped moving. Surprisingly, considering the circumstances, the crowd remained placid throughout. The Belfast News Letter reported:

> The whole scene was awfully impressive. A solemn stillness pervaded the multitude and the utmost order and regularity every where prevailed.

After an hour the bodies were cut down and placed in black-lined coffins provided by relatives. They were carried across the 21-arched Long Bridge (replaced by the Queen's Bridge in 1843) into County Down. Magill and Doe, both of whom left widows and

The solemn cortege carrying the bodies of the
two weavers made its way across the Long Bridge
into County Down (Benn, 1823).

young children, were buried the next afternoon in the one grave at the Knockbreckan burying ground, which lies on the road from Purdysburn to Comber. Perhaps not surprisingly, given the desperate financial plight of their families, no headstone appears to have been erected over the grave.

The melancholy scene was re-enacted the following Friday when another procession left Carrickfergus jail for Belfast with Park and Dickson in a cart along with the executioner. The scaffold was again erected in Castle Place, but not for a hanging but a flogging. The Belfast News Letter recorded:

> *Park was the first who was stripped and tied up, and received 314 lashes which the executioner inflicted with considerable effect. After he was taken down, Dickson underwent a similar punishment, and received 269 lashes. When the whole was finished, they were both re-conducted to jail, where they are to suffer 18 months imprisonment.*

CHAPTER THREE

THE MAKING OF A COUNTY TOWN

They call Belfast the Irish Liverpool;
if people are for calling names, it would
be better to call it the Irish London at
once — the chief city of the kingdom,
at any rate.

William Makepeace Thackeray
(Irish Sketch Book, 1842)

CARRICKFERGUS CASTLE AND TOWN. R.W.522.

Carrickfergus, so long the county town of
Antrim, had to give way to the rapidly growing
Belfast (Welch collection, Ulster Museum).

THERE WERE fewer than 20,000 people living in Belfast at the time of the 1798 Rebellion, and that despite a remarkable growth in the latter half of the 18th century. The industrial revolution, however, triggered an even more spectacular rise in both the town's prosperity and population. In 1811 there were 27,832 souls in Belfast; by 1821 it had grown to more than 37,000; and it leapt to over 53,000 a decade later. The 1841 census recorded 70,447 people living in the town, while the 1851 survey found an additional 17,000. Belfast had surpassed Carrickfergus in importance, though it lacked the official recognition.

The majority of people living in Belfast in the mid-19th century were former farm labourers looking for a better life. In essence the country had came to the town in the hope of finding work, a home and a decent standard of living. Many were to be sorely disappointed. Housing had by no means kept pace with demand and it was not uncommon to find three, four or even five families sharing the one set of rooms. Squalor and misery were everywhere, as were the ale and spirit houses which liberally supplied those who wanted to drown their sorrows in alcohol. The rapid growth in population also saw the arrival of a substantial number of Roman Catholics into what had been predominantly a Protestant town. Belfast had long enjoyed a reputation for religious and political tolerance and was to the forefront in calling for Catholic emancipation. Half the money to build the town's first Roman Catholic church, St Mary's in what is now Chapel Lane, was provided by the Protestants of the town and many were among the congregation at its opening Mass in May, 1784. However, as Belfast's population grew so did sectarian rivalry.

A clear picture of Belfast society at this time is provided through the writings of the Rev William Murphy O'Hanlon, who became minister at the Congregationalist Church in Upper Donegall Street late in 1849. He was shocked by the wretched living standards of the town's poor, their drinking habits, lack of morals and criminal leanings. Mr O'Hanlon was, however, a man who cared and made every effort, through a series of articles in the Northern Whig newspaper which were later reprinted in book form, to make his more fortunate fellow citizens aware of the situation and its consequences. He wrote:

Hulks, penal colonies, and the gallows will never ask in vain for their prey so long as society nurtures such cockatrices's dens as these. We first make our victims, or permit them to be made in our sight, when but by an ordinary measure of exertion would suffice to anticipate the evil; and then, when full-blown, matured, and too strong for ordinary effort to manage and control, we are compelled in self-defence to bring the whole cumbrous and expensive apparatus of punishment to bear upon the evil thus engendered and nursed in our very bosom. We first warm and cherish the serpent, and when it plays the serpent we crush it; we first manufacture our criminals, or sit still while they are manufactured, and then we hang them.

Mr O'Hanlon's arrival in Belfast coincided with the end of a debate on the role of Carrickfergus as the county town of Antrim, or rather which of its rivals might replace it. The growing inadequacies of Carrick's facilities, particularly the limited accommodation in the jail, had become all too obvious.

Given Belfast's rapid growth during the preceding fifty years, it seemed, certainly with hindsight, to be the natural choice as the new county town. However, its success was not straightforward. Antrim and Ballymena were both in the running too. Initially the former seemed the favourite and it took several years of persuasion, and the formation of an influential committee of Belfast's richest and most respected citizens, to swing the case for the town.

The benefits to Belfast were immense. Instead of the town having to pay for the building of its own jail and courthouse, it merely had to contribute 20 per cent of the half-million pounds they cost, with the county paying the rest. By comparison, Belfast was generating more than 70 per cent of the county's criminals. Likewise, the town only paid £1,200 towards the prison's annual running costs of more than £5,500 when it could have been expected to pay, based on the number of Belfast criminals being housed there, some £3,920.

A report presented to the Grand Jury at the opening of the first County Antrim Assizes to be held in the newly-finished courthouse on Thursday, 18th July, 1850, made it clear that Belfast had escaped lightly:

A jail and Court-house have been erected at a cost of above £480,000, Belfast only contributing about one-fifth of the expense, while, for the requirements of the borough, three-fourths of the expenditure became necessary; three-fourths of the number of committals being from Belfast, and it is idle to say, "they are not Belfast men." Had the borough a special jurisdiction, it would be obliged to defray the whole expenses of these offenders.

The former County Courthouse at Carrickfergus
is now the Town Hall and remains one of its
finest buildings

The Grand Jury threatened to introduce a Bill which would separate Belfast from the rest of County Antrim for criminal jurisdiction and fiscal purposes. Such a break did ultimately come about.

While the arguments went on, the fact remained that Belfast was now the county town (it was to be another 38 years before it received its Royal Charter and became a city in 1888) and had a fine prison and courthouse.

As already noted, Belfast was producing the vast majority of the prisoners coming before the County Court. An old jail had existed at Howard Street in the town since 1818, with the Manor Court, the equivalent of a petty sessions, sitting in the building. The more serious criminal element was housed at Carrickfergus, which was neither practical for the constabulary or good for Belfast's self-esteem. Following the completion of the "new House of Correction" on the Crumlin Road in the mid-1840s, two blocks of the old jail were demolished and a proper courthouse built. It was demolished in 1901.

The County Jail was built from black basalt taken from quarries in the hills overlooking the town. Sandstone was imported from Scotland to add the finishing touches. The prison consists of four wings, each with three landings, radiating out from a central hall, and was based on the then recently completed Pentonville Jail. The wings are known by letters, with A-wing to the left if viewing the jail from the Crumlin Road, D-wing to the right next to the Mater Hospital, and B and C wings spaced in between. From the upper floors, the landings look down on to what were open wells. In later years these were covered in wire mesh and partially floored in places to provide recreation areas. It is, in many ways, a traditional Victorian prison, with its design allowing warders to view all four wings from the central hallway. Its main entrance was from the Crumlin Road, through the Governor's House-cum-gate lodge. Work on the jail was begun in 1843 under the watchful eye of County Surveyor Charles Lanyon. By the summer of 1845, and only slightly behind schedule, he was able to tell the Grand Jury that the work was completed, though the jail as yet unoccupied. A debtors jail was added some five years later.

The figure of Justice, on top of the County Antrim Courthouse, was created by Dublin sculptor Boyton Kirk. At one time it was considered to be the finest statue in Belfast (News Letter).

By March, 1846, however, the jail was fully operational and housing some 106 prisoners. Six were awaiting transportation, 17 serving sentences, six of whom were described as "lunatics", and the rest were awaiting trial on a variety of charges, including deserting infant children, rape, larceny, indecent exposure, passing base coins and concealing the birth of a child. Even though most were on what today would be termed remand, all inmates had to wear the prison garb, complete with wooden clogs, and both men and women had their hair cropped to the scalp. Even so, having the Belfast jail in operation was a definite bonus for all concerned. At the opening of the 1846 County Antrim Spring Assizes in Carrickfergus Courthouse, the Hon Justice Crampton was moved to remark: "I am extremely happy to hear that the new House of Correction, erected near Belfast, is answering all the purposes expected from it by those who successfully and benevolently carried out the project."

While the jail might have been bleak and practical, the County Courthouse was considered beautiful. It is difficult to imagine today, given the high density housing which now characterises the area, that the courthouse and jail once stood in the surburbs, with the nearby mountains providing a spectacular backdrop.

Work began on the Lanyon design in 1845. The main contractor was James Carlisle but it is interesting to note that the project brought together Henry McLaughlin and William Harvey as sub-contractors. Later they formed a partnership and the company still bears their name today

The new County Antrim Courthouse, built on the
outskirts of Belfast opposite the County Jail, was
completed in 1850, from about which time this
illustration dates (Ulster Museum).

Atop the courthouse is the figure of Justice, her scales finely balanced. The work of
Dublin sculptor Boyton Kirk, it was said to be the finest statue in the town. Inside, the
Common Hall was some 47 foot square, with a large gallery on one side. Off it led the
entrances to the rest of the building, with the Crown Court occupying the west wing and
the Record Court the east. A tunnel beneath the Crumlin Road connected the court to
the jail opposite, with two chambers for the prisoners to wait in, one for women and the
other men.

The courthouse was enlarged in 1905, with new end blocks added, recesses bricked
up, and a stucco finish applied to the entire building. The amendments destroyed much of
the detail of Lanyon's work.

The completion of the County Courthouse allowed the citizens of Belfast to watch
the arrival of the judges at the opening of each assizes, an event carried out with great
pageantry. The following account, taken from the Belfast News Letter, refers to the
opening of the Summer Assizes of 1910. By then the courthouse held separate hearings
for Belfast and the rest of the county.

> *The Honourable Mr Justice Dodd travelled yesterday morning from
> Newcastle, where he had been staying since the conclusion of the County
> Down Assizes, and arrived in Belfast at ten minutes past eleven o'clock. His
> Lordship was met at the city terminus of the Belfast and County Down*

*Railway by the High Sheriff of County Antrim (Major Montgomery, DC)
and the Under-Sheriff (Mr John R Bristow), with the Under-Sheriff for the
county of Down (Mr Hugh C Kelly). The guard of honour consisted of fifty
non-commissioned officers and men of the 3rd (Reserve) Battalion Royal
Irish Rifles, under Captain A D N Merriman and Lieutenant J B A
Drought, and a detachment of the Royal Irish Constabulary under District-
Inspector Dunlop. The police band, in charge of Mr George C Ferguson, was
also in attendance.*

*The learned Judge, accompanied by the High Sheriff and Under-Sheriff
for the county of Antrim, and escorted by mounted constabulary, drove direct
from the station to the County Courthouse, Crumlin Road; and the High
Sheriff's equipage as it passed through the streets attracted considerable
attention.*

*The Right Honourable Mr Justice Wright, who will open the
commission of Assizes for the county of the city of Belfast tomorrow,
journeyed from Dublin by the train reaching the Great Victoria Street
terminus of the Great Northern Railway at noon. His Lordship was received
on the arrival platform by the High Sheriff of Belfast (Alderman George
Augustus Doran, JP) and the Under-Sheriff (Mr James Quail). The guard
of honour was composed of a detachment of the 3rd (Reserve) Battalion of
the Royal Irish Rifles, and an equal number of constabulary, with band. On
this occasion the carriage in which the learned Judge accompanied by the
High Sheriff and Under-Sheriff, drove from the station to the Courthouse
was an open landau drawn by four splendid bays. The escort consisted of
mounted police. At the Courthouse, both Judges had as a guard of honour a
number of men of the 1st Cheshire Regiment, and on alighting they passed
into the building through a cordon of constabulary.*

The judges arrive by carriage to open the Belfast
and County Antrim Summer Assizes, July 1931.

The map of Belfast in 1888 clearly shows how the
then 43-year-old County Jail's four wings radiate
out from the centre. The County Courthouse,
completed in 1850, stands opposite.

CHAPTER FOUR

LORDS OF THE SCAFFOLD

Come now: the time is short,
Longing to pardon and to bless I wait.
Look up to Me, My sheep so dearly bought,
And say 'Forgive me ere it is too late'.

(from a poem given to the condemned
by executioner James Berry)

The County Antrim jail at Carrickfergus. A beam
protruded from above the top archway, with the
criminal being pushed to his death from the
doorway once the hangman's noose had been
slipped over his head. Such public executions
were abandoned at the jail in 1844, however, after
the hanging of an 18-year-old soldier caused a
public outrage.

FINDING a volunteer to carry out a hanging would seem a daunting prospect, yet there was rarely a shortage of candidates. Even though the post was never advertised, the Home Office received an average of five applications per week from would-be executioners during the first half of the 20th century. Very few, however, ever got the chance to make their appearance on a scaffold.

In spite of the cloak of secrecy surrounding judicial hangings from the late 19th century, when it became the practice to exclude the Press and to limit what serving hangmen were permitted to say, information inevitably seeped out. The custom of recognising one particular man as the chief executioner helped focus the attentions of the newspapers on individuals. Hence many of these "Lords of the Scaffold," such as William Marwood, who began his career in the 1870s, and his successor James Berry became household names in their day, while Albert Pierrepoint is still remembered today, 40 years after he last pushed a trap door lever.

Several of the early hangmen to operate in Belfast, however, not only preferred to remain nameless, but in some cases faceless as well for fear they would be identified by the crowds which gathered to witness their work.

Military courts, operating in the wake of the failed United Irishmen uprising of 1798, condemned at least six rebels to die on the Belfast scaffold. Their executioners were likely to have been soldiers, though in the wake of the uprising it was not unknown for the military authorities to attempt to force civilians to carry out the grisly task. Dr Madden, (Antrim and Down in '98) quotes Dr McGee's account of how General Clavering, "an unprincipled and a merciless man," burned Randalstown after allowing two hours for plunder.

> He proceeded then to Ballymena. One man was ordered for execution; there was no person found to act as executioner; he levied a fine of £50 on the town in consequence, the money was paid, and he then ordered another mulct of £50 to be levied if the head was not struck off and stuck on the market-house. The head was struck off, and the fine was not levied.

The two hangmen who despatched weavers John Doe and John Magill in 1816 came from outside Belfast. One is described as the "usual executioner" from Carrickfergus. The other was "brought from a distant county; he was disguised, having his head and face covered with black crape".

It was prudent for the hangman to remain as anomynous as possible. In England the condemned man, rather than the executioner, was the subject of the crowd's hatred. In Ireland it was often the other way round. Several of the latter-day hangmen felt the need to carry a gun when coming to work in the county jails across the country and often travelled with police guards.

By contrast, the last two executioners at Carrickfergus Jail in the 1840s were apparently well-known in the town. David Strahan, a labourer and one-time prisoner, recalled in March, 1897: "The hangmen at Carrick were Alan McQuilkin and Josey Elliott and they went about openly."

The Press was inclined not to name the man pushing the trap door lever at the early hangings in Belfast, though whether that was by choice or simply because the reporter didn't know the identity is impossible to say. At the execution of soldier Robert O'Neill at Belfast prison in 1854, the Banner of Ulster felt free only to say the hangman "is the same person that officiated in the counties of Armagh, Louth and Monaghan during the past few years".

Even less was given away about the executioner of Daniel Ward in 1863, though his description in the Belfast News Letter certainly deserves mention:

> His stature is small, he appeared to have a hump, and was veiled completely,
> of course . . . The executioner eyed the doomed man with the air of a bull-
> dog, and then stepped in and pinioned him without the slightest resistance.

The newspaper was led to "understand at that moment there was another candidate in the jail for the grim office". The authorities, either as penny-pinching exercises or because of a genuine shortage of outside candidates, sometimes appointed prisoners as executioners, their reward being an early release from the cells. Presumably the disappointed inmate in this case was obliged to complete his sentence.

By the 1870s such a casual approach to the art of hanging was drawing to an end. The Home Office, galvanised into action by a series of botched and embarrassing hangings, was seriously reviewing the procedures and would eventually bring about a uniform approach to executions. At the same time, as Belfast was about to experience, a more enlightened breed of hangman was about to enter the drama enacted on the scaffold.

William Marwood, a cobbler from Horncastle, Lincolnshire, became the main executioner in the British Isles in 1874. Chiefly employed in London, he travelled the country applying his skills and visited Belfast in 1876 to hang the coal porter John Daly. A "tall, stern and determined looking man," he is credited with inventing the 'long drop' method which greatly curtailed the suffering of those ending up on the gallows. By carefully calculating the weight of a condemned man, and gauging the strength of his neck muscles, Marwood created a table of drops whereby the length a felon fell varied. The

James Berry,
EXECUTIONER.

1, BILTON PLACE.
BRADFORD, YORKS.

Hangman James Berry was
proud of his profession and
often handed out calling cards
describing himself as the
"executioner".

James Berry,
Executioner.

Bradford,
Yorkshire.

object, generally achieved, was to break the neck rather than leave the victim to slowly die of strangulation. Marwood, who was over 50 years of age when he took on the job, is also credited with inventing the leather straps used to secure a prisoner's elbows, wrists and knees, and creating a running noose fitted with a metal ring to ensure a smoother despatch.

Among his "clients" were five of the Invincibles involved in the Phoenix Park murders of 1883, when Thomas Henry Burke, Permanent Under-Secretary for Ireland, and Lord Frederick Cavendish, Chief Secretary of State for Ireland, were killed in Dublin.

While Marwood earned the respect of the public, his successor and the next hangman to come to Belfast, was often the butt of ridicule. James Berry, a former policeman and shoe salesman from Bradford, Yorkshire, had caused a sensation in November, 1888 when an execution he was carrying out in Norwich Castle went terribly wrong. Berry miscalculated the drop, giving prisoner Robert Goodale too much rope, resulting in decapitation. In 1891, this time in Liverpool, he almost did the same again, the head remaining barely attached and blood much in evidence. Such incidents were frowned upon by the authorities and seized on by the Press, who made Berry out to be a ghoul.

In 1889, Berry came to Belfast to execute Arthur McKeown for the murder of his common-law wife. As his 10-year-old son played on the gallows while awaiting the arrival of the condemned man, Berry casually gave an interview to a group of reporters, and evidently made a big impression. The Belfast News Letter reported:

47

Berry is not the repulsive individual which reports would lead one to believe. He is a man of medium stature, deep-chested, and strongly knit. In complexion he is sandy, and his beard and whiskers, which are closely cut, are of that peculiar coarseness, indicative of strength. His features are regular, and so far from his countenance being forbidding, were it not for a deep scar extending over a portion of the forehead, and terminating at the right eye, it would be at least pleasing if not inviting. Of his calling he seems to have a more than pardonable pride. A word dropped, a hint however trifling draws from him answers which the legal profession would term speeches. With a peculiar grin, he asserts he has 'pushed off' considerable above one hundred human beings, and that the rope he was that morning using - a tried and trusty Manilla of the Government regulation type, three-quarter inch diameter - had been requisitioned on many previous occasions.

Turning on the charm, Berry - accompanied by an assistant as well as Master Berry - praised the scaffold, saying "he had never seen better in any part of the kingdom". The people of Belfast he thanked for their "intelligence and kindness". Once his work was completed, apparently without a hitch, he left the jail for a few hours sightseeing in Belfast before catching the train to Bangor, returning in time to board the Fleetwood ferry home.

Berry, who invariably carried a gun on his trips to Ireland, believed in confronting a condemned man on the morning of the execution and asking him to confess to his crime before he met his Maker. For a time he was also inclined to pass on to the prisoner, via the chaplain, a copy of a religious poem which he had come across in a newspaper. He was ordered to stop doing this after there were complaints.

The next two executions to be carried out in Belfast were performed by a man named T H Scott, from Huddersfield. Little appears to have been recorded of his career as a hangman, though he is known to have worked as an assistant to Berry on several occasions. Most of Scott's commissions were performed in Ireland and he may have lived in Dublin for a time. In 1894 he came to Belfast to execute farmer John Gilmour, returning seven years later to hang the down-and-out William Woods in 1901. On both occasions he appears to have carried out his task without the aid of an assistant, with no obvious detrimental results.

In between these two Belfast executions he performed a number of others in different parts of Ireland, including the hangings of two men condemned at the 1898 Ulster Winter Assizes, which sat in Belfast in December. Co Cavan murderers Thomas Kelly and Philip King were executed respectively on 10th and 13th January, 1899 at Armagh Jail. A third man sentenced to death by the same court was reprieved and later taken from Derry Jail to Mountjoy Prison, Dublin, to serve his sentence. Scott, who had already hanged a man at Kilkenny Jail earlier that month, was assisted on all three occasions by Batholomew Binns, who had briefly followed Marwood as the principal State executioner until he was removed because, as one prison governor put it, he "had no idea how to do his work properly".

E/.   20th March, 1933.

Dear Sir,

     Harold Courtney was at Armagh Assizes
on Saturday last convicted of the Murder of Minnie
Reid, and was sentenced to death, and to be hanged
at <u>Belfast Prison</u> on Friday, 7th April 1933.

     Will you please wire me on the enclosed
Form if you can act as Executioner on this occasion.
Wire Yes or No on the enclosed Form, and sign your
name "Legal".

     In addition to sending me the Wire you
will please write me confirming your Wire to me, and
further stating if you have any other executions during
that week beginning 3rd April, and if any, where?

     If I engage you as Executioner, also
state in your letter what route you will travel to
Belfast. You would have to travel not later than
Wednesday, 5th April, arriving in Belfast not later
than Thursday, 6th April.

     Send me Wire at once, and write also to
me to-morrow, Tuesday.

            Yours faithfully,

            Under-sheriff,Co. Armagh

Mr. Thomas W. Pierrepoint,
    Town End,
       Clayton,
          Near Bradford,
            Yorkshire.   ENGLAND.

Copies of some of the many letters sent by
Armagh Under-Sheriff Valentine Wilson to
executioner Thomas Pierrepoint in the run-up
to Harold Countney's hanging
(Public Record Office).

24th March, 1933.

Dear Sir,

Re Harold Courtney.

I am in receipt of yours of the 22nd inst.
received this morning, and if you are personally
present at the execution I have no objection to
your nephew, Albert Pierrepoint, acting as your
Assistant. Of course, if through any unforeseen
accident or illness on your part you cannot attend,
I would prefer to have another person on the List
who has experience of carrying out executions acting
as the Principal, but in any case with your nephew as
Assistant.   You will kindly please communicate with
your Assistant, Albert Pierrepoint, and get him to
write me at once accepting the position.   I
suppose your Assistant will travel with you to
Heysham, and that you both will proceed from Heysham
together.   I believe the boat leaves Heysham at
eleven o'clock for Belfast, and you might please
let me know what train you will catch from Bradford,
and if it is a boat train.

I will write you further next week.

Kindly acknowledge receipt.

Yours faithfully,

Under-sheriff, Co. Armagh.

Mr. Thos. W. Pierrepoint,
    Town End,
        Clayton,
            Nr. Bradford,

            Yorks, ENGLAND.

E/.

Dear Sir,

Re Harold Courtney

I am in receipt of yours of yesterday's date. I do not think there will be any reprieve in this case, as the Lord Chief Justice in passing sentence was very strong against any such hope.

I note that you will leave Bradford at 9p.m. on Wednesday night, and I herewith enclose you a Form of Telegram stamped, which kindly despatch to me. On no account sign your name, as I prefer your movements to be kept secret.

I have had a letter this morning from your nephew stating that he is travelling by the 9.5 train from Manchester, and will meet you at Heysham. I enclose you my cheque for £4. on a/c., and if you do not require to cash this before leaving I will give you the cash when in Belfast. I think you should despatch the above wire about 8.45p.m. on Wednesday night.

Kindly acknowledge receipt of cheque.

Yours faithfully,

Under-sheriff, Co. Armagh.

Mr. Thos. W. Pierrepoint,
    Town End,
        Clayton,
            Nr. Bradford,
                Yorks., England.

In 1909 the most famous name among modern executioners, that of Pierrepoint, appeared in Belfast for the first time in person. The occasion was the hanging of Richard Justin, one of 19 executions Harry Pierrepoint carried out that year. In his black-bound Execution Book, in which he noted the birth of his children, the addresses of assistant executioners, and cures for cow coughs as well as the details of the men he hanged, he recorded his expenses for the trip - £1 11s 3d was his fare to Belfast, plus a shilling for the cab.

Harry was the first of a dynasty which was to last almost to the end of hanging itself in Britain. Another Yorkshireman, he applied for the job of hangman when he was just 25, and assisted at his first execution in 1901. He apparently enjoyed his work and, unlike his companions, was inclined to celebrate afterwards. It was common practice for him to head for the pub immediately he came out of a prison after completing an execution. Sometimes his drinking binges lasted up to a week. It seems likely, judging by comments made by subsequent family members who took up the profession, that he was also fond of a drink or two before an execution.

An unusual feature of Harry Pierrepoint's term as executioner was his habit of placing the noose around the prisoner's neck before pulling on the white hood. It was generally more usual to do it the other way round, so saving the condemned man from the feel of the rope on his skin and reducing the likelihood of visible injuries to the neck. Harry resigned as hangman in 1914, by which time his older brother, Thomas, was well established as an executioner. But before the Pierrepoint name was to reappear in Belfast, another famous, and tragic, executioner was to be called to the city.

John Ellis was coming towards the end of his hanging career, which had spanned almost a quarter of a century, when he accepted the call to execute child killer Simon McGeown in 1924. From a respectable Rochdale family, he incurred the wrath of his father when he applied for the post but, despite threats of being disowned, pressed on, being accepted on to the list of approved hangmen in 1901. He was a man singularly unsuited to such a profession and suffered from a nervous condition which at times caused a form of virtual stage fright. Nonetheless, his career progressed and in 1907 he was competent enough to be selected to act as the Number One executioner for the first time.

Over the next two decades he was to be associated with some of the most infamous executions of this century, including the hanging of American murderer Dr Hawley Harvey Crippen in 1910. Six years later it was Sir Roger Casement, who had been convicted of treason, who was to feel Ellis' rope about his neck. Casement, who had enjoyed a highly successful career in the Foreign Office, had spent the early years of the First World War in Germany, where he attempted to establish an Irish Brigade by recruiting prisoners of war to fight the British. Later, after negotiating German support for the planned 1916 uprising, he travelled to Ireland by U-Boat, but was arrested virtually as he set foot ashore. Convicted at the Old Bailey of treason, he was hanged by Ellis at Pentonville on 3rd August, 1916.

The Casement affair was by no means the end of Ellis' connection with Irish politics, and he returned time and again to execute those condemned to death as a result of the violence which consumed Ireland following the end of the war and partition.

In 1923, another celebrated case came Ellis' way. Edith Thompson, along with her young lover Frederick Bywaters, was condemned to be hanged for murdering her husband. The execution caused a public outcry, which was later inflamed by reports of the poor physical and mental state of the woman in her final days and hours. All those involved in the hanging, including Ellis, were said to have been badly affected by the experience.

Many have claimed since that it was Mrs Thompson's execution which finally prompted Ellis to resign as hangman in 1924, having carried out in excess of 200 killings. Within a few months he attempted suicide, but only managed to wound himself with the gun. In September, 1932, after taking a few drinks, he succeeded in taking his own life by slitting his throat with a razor.

The next hangman to utilise the Crumlin Road scaffold was William Willis, who had acted as assistant to Ellis at the hanging of McGeown. His return, this time as the Number One, came two years later for the execution of Michael Pratley in 1924. Although he acted as the chief executioner in a handful of hangings in Great Britain, including that of Mrs Thompson's lover Bywaters, his career was primarily confined to that of assistant hangman. By the time he retired from the gallows he had been in attendance at more than 100 hangings.

Another Pierrepoint appeared in Belfast in 1928, this time in the form of Thomas, brother of the aforementioned Harry. Thomas Pierrepoint, however, was a different kind of person, and was to become by far Belfast's most regular hangman, monopolising executions in the city up to the Second World War. His first victim was Smiley, followed in 1930 by Cushnan, 1931 Dornan, 1932 Cullens, 1933 Courtney and Willians in 1942.

Thomas is said to have sucked sweets as he prepared the prisoners for the drop and obviously tackled his task in a detached and workmanlike manner. He is estimated to have carried out more than 300 hangings in total in a career which continued up until 1946, when he retired aged 73.

Harry's son Albert began his apprenticeship as hangman by assisting his uncle Thomas in Dublin in 1931. Albert, who is the best remembered of modern hangmen, never got to practice his craft in the Province as chief executioner. He numbered Ruth Ellis and Derek Bentley, who was later posthumously reprieved, among his victims.

While in Great Britain the Home Office selected assistants, in Northern Ireland it was left to the High Sheriff to arrange. For the most part, the authorities were willing to accept Thomas' suggestion that Albert come along as his number two. It was this pairing which hanged Harold Courtney in 1933. The correspondence between Pierrepoint and the Under-Sheriff of Armagh, Valentine Wilson, reveals the secrecy involved in employing an executioner, and the security measures taken. Notable in the letter below is the query about any other executions that week. The hangmen were inclined to accept all jobs which came their way, even if the dates clashed, in the belief that at least one of the condemned would be reprieved.

The authorities, embarrassed by the bad publicity
generated by some of those on the approved list
of hangmen, issued a number of memorandum to
ensure that everyone knew what was expected
from the executioners (Public Record Office).

To be submitted to the High Sheriff.

Memorandum of Conditions to which any Person acting as Executioner is required to conform.

1. Every person acting as executioner is required to conform to any instructions he may receive from or on behalf of the High Sheriff as to the day and hour and route for going to and leaving the place of execution.

2. He is required to report himself at the prison at which an execution it to take place, and for which he has been engaged, not later than 4 o'clock on the afternoon preceding the day of execution.

3. He is required to remain in the prison from the time of his arrival until he has completed the execution, and until permission is given him to leave.

4. During the time he remains in the prison he will be provided with lodging and maintenance.

5. By desire of the Secretary of State the supply of articles for maintenance while residing in the prison will be subject to necessary restrictions to ensure moderation, and the daily supply of alcoholic liquor to each person will be limited as under :—

$$1 \text{ quart of malt liquor} \left\{ \begin{array}{l} 1 \text{ pint at dinner,} \\ 1 \text{ pint at supper.} \end{array} \right.$$

or

½ pint of spirit.

6. He should clearly understand that his conduct and general behaviour should be respectable, not only at the place and time of the execution, but before and subsequently; that he should avoid attracting public attention in going to or from the prison, and he is prohibited from giving to any person particulars on the subject of his duty for publication.

7. His remuneration will be £ *10* for the performance of the duty required of him, to which will be added £ *5* if his conduct and behaviour are satisfactory, during and subsequent to, the execution. These fees will not be payable until a fortnight after the execution has taken place.

8. Records will be kept of his conduct and efficiency on each occasion of his being employed, and this record will be at the disposal of any High Sheriff who may have to engage an executioner.

9. The name of any person who does not give satisfaction, or whose conduct is in any way objectionable, so as to cast discredit on himself, either in connexion with the duties or otherwise, will be removed from the list.

10. The necessary ropes, straps, pinioning apparatus, cap, &c., will be provided at the prison, and must not be removed therefrom.

11. The executioner will give such information or make such record of the occurrence as the Governor of the prison may require.

November, 1907.

3 DEC 1932

MINISTRY OF HOME AFFAIRS

t (2)18266 Pk 13 150 8/22 E & S

4

Enclosure No. 2.

(Copy.)

Whitehall, 7th October, 1885.

SIR,

I AM directed by the Secretary of State to acquaint you that on several recent occasions his attention has been called to the proceedings, before and after an execution, of the person employed as executioner, which appear to have given rise to grave public scandal.

The Secretary of State thinks that the danger of the repetition of such occurences would be much diminished if it could be arranged that, on the occasion of every execution, the executioner should reside in the prison while he is in the place where the execution takes place. The Secretary of State has, of course, no authority to control the movements of the executioner who is engaged and paid solely by the Sheriff, as the officer solely responsible for the carrying out of the execution; but the Secretary of State has, as you are aware, already given instructions that quarters should be provided for the executioner in the prison, whenever the Sheriff wishes him to reside there, and he thinks that it is desirable that in future, when it is known that an execution is about to take place in any prison, the Governor should be instructed at once to communicate with the Sheriff and inform him that, if he so desires, the executioner will be provided with lodging and maintenance in the prison, and that, in the opinion of the Secretary of State, he should, in engaging the executioner, make it compulsory that he should sleep there so long as he may remain in the place where the sentence is to be executed, and certainly on the night preceding the execution.

The Sheriff should, of course understand that this matter is one entirely for his discretion, but that the Secretary of State, while not wishing to interfere with his responsibility, desires him to be informed of his opinion that grave public scandals may be avoided by insisting on this as a condition in the engagement of the executioner.

I am, &c.

(Signed)   GODFREY LUSHINGTON.

The Chairman of
The Prison Commissioners,
    &c.   &c.   &c.

5

Enclosure No. 3.

MEMORANDUM on the subject of EXECUTIONS.

In continuation of Memoranda issued by the Secretary of State in
October, 1885.

1. With a view to assisting the High Sheriffs in the selection and
appointment of suitable persons to carry out executions, the Secretary of
State has decided that a small list of persons who have acted in, or are
believed to be willing and competent to undertake, the office of executioner,
shall be kept at the Home Office. Records will be kept of their conduct
and efficiency on each occasion of their being employed, and the information
thus recorded will be at the disposal of any High Sheriff who may have to
engage an executioner. The name of any person who does not give satisfaction, or whose conduct is in any way objectionable, so as to cast discredit
on himself, either in connection with the duties or otherwise, will be removed
from the list.

2. When an execution is about to take place the list of names and
addresses, and the necessary information from the record kept as above,
will be sent to the Governor of the prison for the information of the High
Sheriff, and it will be left to the High Sheriff to engage one of them if he
thinks fit to do so.

3. The Committee appointed in 1886 to inquire into and to report upon
the subject of the carrying out of capital sentences were of opinion that it is
very important and desirable that there should be an assistant to the executioner, " who might gradually acquire experience, might assist where several
" criminals were simultaneously executed, or might replace the executioner
" when he was ill, or when his presence was required in different places at the
" same time." Sanction has been obtained for the employment of such
assistants at the public expense, and the Governor may, if the High Sheriff
concurs, engage one or more persons to be present at the execution in order
to gain practical experience and to act as assistants if required under the
orders of the High Sheriff. The provisions in regard to accommodating the
executioner in the prison, and to his conduct in connection with the execution
and before and after it, will apply also to any assistant who may be so engaged.
It must, however, be clearly understood, that the engagement of assistants by
the Governor does not take away from the High Sheriff or his deputy or the
executioner appointed by him any of the responsibility attaching to the offices
they respectively fulfil.

4. Besides the suggestions contained in the letter from the Home Office,
dated 7th October, 1885, the Secretary of State thinks it desirable to express
his opinion that executioners should be made clearly to understand that their
conduct and general behaviour should be respectable not only at the place
and time of execution, but before and subsequently: that they should
avoid attracting public attention in going to or from it, and that they should
be prohibited from giving interviews for publication to any persons on the
subject of their duty. This end would be better secured by their remuneration not being payable till a fortnight after the execution, and the payment
of a part of it being made dependent upon their satisfactory behaviour.

5. The Secretary of State suggests that the persons engaged should be
required to conform to any instructions they may receive from or on behalf of
the High Sheriff as to the day and hour and route for going to and leaving the
place of execution.

6. It is suggested that the persons should be required to undertake to
report themselves at the prison at which an execution is to take place, and for
which they have been engaged, not later than 4 o'clock on the afternoon
preceding the day of execution ; also that they should remain in the prison
from the time of their arrival until they have completed the execution and
until permission is given them to leave.

A 3.

6

7. With a view to carrying out the objects referred to in paragraphs 1 and 2 as to the record to be kept of the conduct and efficiency of the person or persons employed as executioner or assistant, High Sheriffs are requested to be good enough to make a report to the Home Office in regard to the manner in which the duty has been performed on each occasion. Reports as to their conduct, character, and efficiency will also be made by the Governor, &c. These reports will be recorded at the Home Office, and the information they afford will (as stated in paragraph 1) be placed at the disposal of any High Sheriff who has to appoint an executioner.

8. Straps, pinioning apparatus, &c., and ropes will be put at the disposal of the High Sheriff with and on the same conditions as the rest of the apparatus referred to in the memorandum issued in 1885. They will be available at the prison.

9. A memorandum of " Conditions to which any person acting as " executioner is required to conform," having reference to the terms of his engagement and his personal conduct ; also a memorandum of " Instructions " for carrying out the details of an execution " have been furnished to the Governors of prisons for the assistance of the High Sheriff if he thinks it desirable to adopt them, when he becomes responsible for the carrying out of an execution.

10. The Secretary of State wishes it to be clearly understood that the suggestions made in this memorandum are not intended in any way to interfere with or diminish the responsibility of the High Sheriff attaching to him by Statute, and in particular that, from the moment when the condemned prisoner is handed over to him, the executioner acts entirely under the Sheriff's orders, and that the Sheriff is alone responsible for his conduct and for his treatment of the prisoner, e.g., in allowing or refusing to allow him to make any statement, or to speak with the Chaplain.

Home Office, Whitehall, December, 1891.

N.B.—As soon as the High Sheriff has fixed a date for an execution he should officially inform the Home Office.

The letter to Pierrepoint, dated 20th March, 1933, reads:

Dear sir,

Harold Courtney was at Armagh Assizes on Saturday last convicted of the murder of Minnie Reid, and was sentenced to death, and to be hanged at Belfast Prison on Friday, 7th April, 1933.

Will you please wire me on the enclosed form if you can act as executioner on this occasion. Wire Yes or No on the enclosed form, and sign your name "Legal".

In addition to sending me the wire you will please write me confirming your wire to me, and further stating if you have any other executions during that week beginning 3rd April, and if any, where?

If I engage you as executioner also state in your letter what route you will travel to Belfast. You would have to travel not later than Wednesday, 5th April, arriving in Belfast not later than Thursday, 6th April.

Send me wire at once, and write also to me tomorrow, Tuesday.

Yours faithfully, Under-Sheriff, Co Armagh

Thomas wrote back and as usual suggested Albert as assistant executioner. His nephew was then new to the official list of trained hangmen and would have been unknown to Mr Wilson. Nonetheless, the Under-Sheriff agreed to Pierrepoint's request, but with the rider: "Of course, if through any unforeseen accident or illness on your part you cannot attend, I would prefer to have another person on the List who has experience of carrying out executions acting as the principal, but in any case with your nephew as assistant".

Belfast police commissioner F A Britten was also told of the hangmen's arrangements and asked:

I would feel grateful if you would arrange to have a constable in plain clothes on arrival of Heysham Boat on Thursday, 6th April, to see these two men to the Gaol at Belfast, and also to see them depart from Belfast on the Heysham Boat on Friday night, 7th April.

The arrival and departure of the Executioner and his Assistant should be kept strictly private.

The Commissioner, of course, obliged. Meanwhile, Mr Wilson was making arrangements with Pierrepoint in the event of a reprieve. It was not unknown for a prankster, or anti-hanging activist, to try to sabatoge proceedings.

If there should be a reprieve, and I have to wire you, will you kindly note that my wire will be signed "Valentine Wilson" with the word "Seal" immediately after. Remember, the word "Seal" must be on the telegram to you to show that it has my authority.

31st March, 1933.

Dear Sir,

Harold Courtney, a Prisoner, is to be executed in Belfast Prison on Friday, 7th April 1933, for the murder of Minnie Reid.

I have appointed Thomas W. Pierrepoint as Executioner, with Albert Pierrepoint as his Assistant. They will travel via Heysham, and arrive in Belfast on Thursday morning, 6th April. I would feel grateful if you would arrange to have a Constable in plain clothes on arrival of Heysham Boat on Thursday, 6th April, to see these two men to the Gaol at Belfast, and also to see them depart from Belfast on the Heysham Boat on Friday night, 7th April.

The arrival and departure of the Executioner and his Assistant should be kept strictly private.

Thanking you in anticipation.

Yours faithfully,

Under-sheriff, Co. Armagh.

F. A. Britten Esq., O.B.E.
    Commissioner of Police,
        Police Office,
            Chichester St.,
                BELFAST.

While confidentiality was sought at all levels to ensure the safe arrival and departure of the executioners, the RUC was still asked to be on hand to escort the men to and from the jail (Public Record Office).

COMMISSIONER'S OFFICE,

ROYAL ULSTER CONSTABULARY,

BELFAST,

3rd April 19 33.

PERSONAL.

Sir,

I have received your letter of 31st ult, with reference to the execution of Harold Courtney at Belfast Gaol on 7th inst. The necessary arrangements will be made with regard to the arrival and departure of the executioners.

I am, Sir,
Your obedient servant,

J. a. Britten

COMMISSIONER.

Valentine Wilson, Esq.,
48 Church Street,
Portadown,
Co. Armagh.

In the event it was not to be. A telegram despatched following a Cabinet meeting at Stormont on 5th April, and signed by the Minister of Home Affairs, gave the execution the green light.

> *Case of Harold Courtney has received careful consideration. Cabinet of Northern Ireland have failed to discover any grounds which would justify them in advising his Grace the Governor to interfere with the due course of the law. His Grace has accordingly decided that the law must take its course.*

The Under-Sheriff later put in a bill to the Ministry of Home Affairs for £29 14s, including £5 2s incurred by himself for hiring a car to get him to and from Crumlin Road Jail because there was a rail strike at the time. The authorities declined to meet this extra expense.

The rest of the bill broke down as follows:

	£	s	p
Executioner's fee	12	–	–
Fare from Bradford to Belfast	2	15	–
Cabs		9	–
Subsistence allowance		10	–
Assistant executioner's fee	4	–	–
Fare from Manchester to Belfast	2	10	–
Cabs		8	–
Subsistence allowance		10	–
Portadown Times A/c for printing	1	10	–

Pierrepoint senior received an advance of £10, with another £2 being sent on later if it was decided "his conduct and behaviour are satisfactory, during and subsequent to, the execution". Not a great deal of money by any standards.

The printing bill was for the production of declaration forms, to be nailed outside the prison, initially announcing the execution was to take place and later that it had been carried out according to the law.

Albert Pierrepoint, who ran a pub when not operating a scaffold, became the first-choice executioner in Britain following his uncle's retirement, but never returned to the Province. He resigned in February, 1956, ending the Pierrepoint's 55-year reign. Albert, who was normally armed on his trips across the Irish Sea, later claimed a staggering 550 hangings, including large numbers of war criminals - five times his father's total.

Following the Pierrepoints' exit from the scene, two men - Les Stewart and Harry Allen - were jointly made the Number One executioners. It was the latter who brought hangings in Belfast to an end when he came to Northern Ireland twice in 1961.

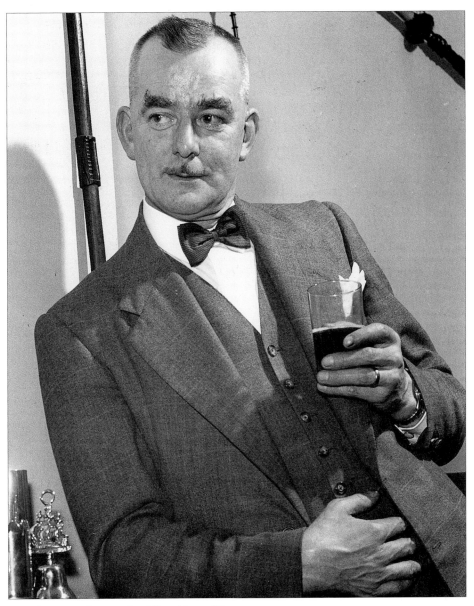

Part-time executioner and publican Harry Allen,
who cut a fine dash in his three-piece suit and
bow tie, carried out the last two hangings carried
out in Northern Ireland
(Press Association).

Allen, from Manchester and also a publican, had spent many years in Pierrepoint's shadow. He was already considered one of the most senior assistants at least a decade before his big chance came and had performed a number of executions as the chief man. Syd Dernley, an assistant hangman who worked on occasions with Allen during the 1940s, had mixed feelings about him. On one occasion the pair, along with another assistant also called Harry Allen, came together for a double execution at Wandsworth prison. Dernley recalled:

> The Manchester Harry Allen seemed a cheerful type, if a little flamboyant; I could scarcely believe the bow tie! He was friendly enough, in a condescending way that announced that he was the senior assistant and we were mere newcomers.

Stewart and Allen were to carry out the last two executions in Britain. Peter Anthony Allen was hanged at Walton Prison, Liverpool, by Stewart and Gwynne Owen Evans by Allen at Strangeways Jail, Manchester. Both were carried out on 13th August, 1964.

CHAPTER FIVE

UNTIL YOU ARE DEAD

*I think it is quick, certain and humane.
I think it is the fastest and quickest in
the world bar nothing. It is quicker than
shooting, and cleaner*

Executioner Albert Pierrepoint
(On the merits of hanging)

Northern Ireland Spring Assizes, 1933.

County of Armagh — To Wit

By the Lords Justices of Assize for the Circuit of Northern Ireland at a General Assizes, Session of Oyer and Terminer, and General Gaol Delivery held at Armagh in and for said County on Monday the Thirteenth day of March, 1933.

Whereas, Harold Courtney late of Church Street, Dungannon, in the County of Tyrone was at the said Assizes in due form of Law, indicted, tried, and convicted that between the 26th day of July, 1932, and the 4th day of August, 1932, at Derryane in the County of Armagh aforesaid he feloniously wilfully and of his malice aforethought did kill and murder one Minnie Reid against the Peace of our Lord the King his Crown and Dignity, and thereupon Judgment was given by the Court that the said Harold Courtney be taken from the Bar of the Court where he now stands to the Prison whence he last came and that on Friday the Seventh day of April in the year of our Lord One thousand nine hundred and thirty three be be taken to the common place of execution in the Prison in which he shall be then confined, and then and there hanged by the neck till he be dead and that his body be buried within the precincts of the Prison in which the aforesaid judgment of death shall be executed upon him.

And it was ordered by the Court that execution of the said Judgment be done upon him in manner and form aforesaid on Friday the Seventh day of April, One thousand nine hundred and thirty-three.

These are therefore in His Majesty's name strictly to charge and command you the Sheriff of the said County of Armagh in whose custody in His Majesty's Gaol at Belfast the said Harold Courtney now remains that you repair to the said Gaol and thereout take the body of the said Harold Courtney and that you cause execution of the Judgment aforesaid to be done upon the said Harold Courtney in manner and form as above set forth on Friday the Seventh day of April, One thousand nine hundred and thirty-three, and for your so doing this shall be your sufficient Warrant.

Sealed with my Seal of Office and dated this First day of April One thousand nine hundred and thirty-three.

By the Court

Henry J. Mann

Clerk of the Crown and Peace for the said County of Armagh

To
The Sheriff of the County of Armagh
and his Assistants.

ALTHOUGH the ultimate objective was always the same – to 'hang by the neck until dead' – the ritual and methods of execution have varied over the centuries. Where, when and how a condemned man died was once the preserve of the courts, with the finer details added by the individual hangmen. Often a judge favoured taking a culprit to either the scene of his crime or even his own front door to meet his fate, the object being to set an example to the prisoners' friends and relatives. In such instances, a temporary scaffold was erected at the chosen place of execution or a convenient tree employed.

By the time executions became routine in Belfast, however, the pattern had become well established if not entirely formalised. Following the abandonment of public hangings, the Home Office formally outlined how a criminal convicted of a capital offence was to meet his end, while still leaving the High Sheriff as the responsible party.

In 1885 a series of documents were issued from Whitehall which, although added to and occasionally altered, provided the basis for executions for the next 80 years. Copies of these papers were dispensed to the County Sheriffs by the governor of Belfast Prison once an inmate had been convicted of a capital offence. What the documents basically did was tell the Sheriff, as if he were in any doubt, that he was "solely responsible for carrying into effect the sentence of death, and for this purpose, or for any purpose relating thereto, having by statute the control over the prisons and the officers thereof". He was invited to inspect the gallows and prison facilities with a view to making any alterations he felt necessary. At least part of an executioner's pay, he was advised, should be retained for a couple of weeks after the hanging to ensure the hangman's good behaviour before, during and after the event.

A warrant, issued by the court to the Sheriff and his assistants, gave them the legal right to have a prisoner, in this case Harold Courtney, "hanged by the neck until he be dead" (Public Record Office).

On a more general note, the Sheriff was asked to ensure that the execution took place during the week following the third Sunday after the day on which the sentence was passed, on any weekday bar a Monday; that a public notice, stating the date and time of execution, be posted on the prison gate; and that the prison bell be tolled for 15 minutes after the hanging.

In practice, the prison Trades Staff at Crumlin Road tested the equipment before the executioner and his assistant arrived, which was normally on the afternoon prior to the hanging. The hangmen, after depositing their overnight bags in their room, would be taken to the scaffold. At this point they would usually stop on the way to peer at the condemned man through the peep hole in the cell door to assess his build. For this purpose the warders had their charge sitting at the table playing cards or some other game, with either his back or side view to the door. The alternative was to take the condemned man out for some fresh air in the exercise yard, allowing the executioner to view him from a distance. In either case, it was felt important that the prisoner was not aware that he was being assessed for the grim business the next morning.

Once in the execution room, there was a short delay while the executioners waited until the prisoner had been taken from the cell, usually to the chapel or exercise yard, so there was no danger of him over-hearing the preparations. The rigging of the apparatus was comparatively simple. All the necessary equipment was supplied by the Home Office and came in two black wooden boxes, one larger than the other. From the smaller box, which also included pulley blocks, the executioner removed a length of chain. With the aid of a step-ladder, this was attached to the cross-beam.

The larger box contained two ropes, linen hoods, straps, copper wire, thread and chalk. One of the ropes (often one was brand new while the other had already been used several times), was shackled to the end of the chain, having first been marked with the required length of drop. The drop was calculated by dividing the man's weight in pounds by 1,000, and converting the answer into feet and inches. A Table of Drops was provided, of course, but at the end of the day it was at the executioner's discretion whether he went for the recommended distance or added or subtracted inches according to his assessment of the prisoner's build and allowing for age. By adjusting the chain, the mark on the rope was set at head height. The rope's slack was then taken up in a series of loops, which were held together with thread from the box, leaving the noose hanging at the right height to slip over the condemned man's head. The noose itself was covered in leather to minimise the amount of visible damage caused to the neck, and worked by running through a brass eye. After being attached it was held in place by a rubber or leather washer.

Enclosures sent to the Sheriff, or Under-Sheriff,
outlining his duties, which included organising an
executioner and ensuring the scaffold was up to
standard (Public Record Office).

H.M. Prison.

19

SIR,

IN obedience to instructions I beg leave to acquaint you that prisoner

has been received into my custody under sentence of death, and to forward, for your information, copies of the under-mentioned Memoranda, &c., in reference to the carrying out of executions :

Enclosure No. 1.—Memorandum of instructions on the subject of executions issued by the Secretary of State in 1885.

Enclosure No. 2.—Letter dated 7th October 1885 from the Secretary of State to the Prison Commissioners.

Enclosure No. 3.—Further memorandum on the subject of executions issued by the Secretary of State, and dated December 1891.

Enclosure No. 4.—Memorandum of conditions to which it is suggested that any person acting as executioner should be required to conform. (Two loose copies of this memorandum are enclosed for transmission to the person whom you may engage as executioner in case you should require him to conform to the conditions therein laid down— one copy may be retained by him for guidance and the other returned to you with a signed acknowledgment thereon that he will conform to the conditions.)

Enclosure No. 5.—List of candidates reported as competent for the office of executioner.

Enclosure No. 6.—A copy of the rules made by the Secretary of State, pursuant to the provisions of the Capital Punishment Amendment Act, 1868, for regulating the execution of capital sentences.

I am further to inform you that I have in my keeping a " Memorandum of instructions for carrying out the details of an execution," also a " Table of Drops." These instructions will be available for the guidance of the executioner while in the prison, should you desire him to adopt them, and if you wish it, I will forward these documents to you for your personal perusal, but I am directed to request that you will kindly return them to me in accordance with the note thereon.

I am, Sir,

Your obedient Servant,

Prof Stephenson
Governor.

Under
To the ~~High~~ Sheriff

No. 275.

r (2)18162 Pk 12 100 7/22 E & S   A

3

Enclosure No. 1.

MEMORANDUM of INSTRUCTIONS on the subject of EXECUTIONS, issued
by the SECRETARY OF STATE in 1885.

The Sheriff being solely responsible for carrying into effect the sentence
of death, and for this purpose, or for any purpose relating thereto, having
by statute the control over the prisons and the officers thereof, whenever
a Governor receives a prisoner under sentence of death he is forthwith to
inform the Sheriff of the fact, and to specify what means exist at the time in
the prison for carrying out the sentence.

The Governor will invite the Sheriff to inspect the apparatus and to test
its operation ; so as to satisfy himself of its efficiency in every respect.

He is also to inquire of the Sheriff whether he desires any works to be
done in the prison, either to improve the apparatus or to facilitate the
carrying out of the execution, and if the Sheriff answers in the affirmative
the Governor is to inform him that the responsibility rests with him, and that
he is at liberty, and it is his duty, to select and employ at his discretion
proper workmen, and to direct them to carry out such works as he thinks
necessary, but that the Prison Commissioners will offer all requisite facilities
and will, if requested in due time, place at his disposal all such labour
and materials as they have at their command free of cost (unless otherwise
notified to him).

8

Enclosure No. 6.

RULES made by HIS MAJESTY'S PRINCIPAL SECRETARY OF STATE for the HOME DEPARTMENT, pursuant to the provisions of the Capital Punishment Amendment Act, 1868, for regulating the execution of CAPITAL SENTENCES.

1. For the sake of uniformity it is recommended that Executions should take place in the week following the third Sunday after the day on which the sentence is passed, on any week day but Monday, and at 8 a.m.

2. The mode of execution and the ceremonial attending it to be the same as heretofore in use.

3. A Public Notice, under the hands of the Sheriff and the Governor of the Prison, of the date and hour appointed for the execution to be posted on the Prison Gate not less than twelve hours before the execution, and to remain until the inquest has been held.

4. The Bell of the Prison, or if arrangements can be made for that purpose, the Bell of the Parish or other neighbouring Church, to be tolled for 15 minutes after the execution.

5. The person or persons engaged to carry out the execution should be required to report themselves at the Prison not later than 4 o'clock on the afternoon preceding the execution, and to remain in the Prison from the time of their arrival until they have completed the execution and until permission is given them to leave.

Approved by the
Secretary of State,
Whitehall,
5th June, 1902.

Next the hangmen, using a tape measure, calculated exactly the centre of the trap doors, marking the point with a chalked 'T'. Unless the prisoner was stopped on exactly the right spot, he would end up swinging back and forth when dropped. When in the right position, however, the body hung virtually motionless. A "dummy" run with a sand bag acting as the body was then carried out, often in front of the prison governor, engineering officer and the High Sheriff or his representative. Everyone then left the execution room, the door being locked behind them. The sand bag was left hanging overnight to ensure the rope was fully stretched.

I, PATRICK E. O'FLAHERTY, the Surgeon of H.M. Prison at Belfast, hereby Certify that I this day examined the body of Harold Courtney, on whom Judgment of death was this day executed in the Prison, Belfast, and that on examination I found that the said Harold Courtney was dead.

Dated this 7th April, 1933.

Within minutes of an execution, notices were placed on the prison door confirming for the crowds normally gathered outside that the sentence of death had been carried out (Public Record Office).

We, the undersigned, declare that Judgment of death was this day executed on Harold Courtney in the Prison, Belfast, in our presence.

Dated this 7th April, 1933.

Valentine Webst

Under Sheriff of County Armagh.

Row Stephenson

Governor of H.M. Prison, Belfast.

The hangmen retired to their room for tea and a long and tense evening playing cards, reading or chatting. Early next morning they returned to the scaffold to remove the sand bag, reset the trap doors, and check the preparations of the previous evening. With any adjustments carried out, and the noose again tied up at head height, the Number One and his assistant retired to await the call. A few minutes before 8am, the executioners were conducted back to the condemned cell by a warder. The official party would already be in position to one side of the scaffold. This group, although sometimes varying in size, always contained the prison governor or his deputy, the medical officer, and the High Sheriff or his representative.

At the stroke of 8am, both men entered the condemned cell and quickly walked up to the prisoner, who was stripped to his shirt with his neck bared, He would be deliberately seated with his back to the entrance, usually engaged in prayers with the chaplain. Tapping him on the shoulder to get him to stand, the chief executioner bound his arms behind his back. Turning, he led the way on to the scaffold, the prisoner following with the two prison warders close at hand and the assistant and padre bringing up the rear. The Number One stopped the man on the trap doors, positioning him on the T marked earlier. As he pulled the white hood over the man's head, followed by the rope, the assistant bound the legs with a leather strap. The metal eye of the noose was placed under the jaw, slightly to the left, with the intention of breaking the neck between the first, second or third cervical vertebrae. The spinal cord was also likely to be destroyed, either being crushed or torn from the brain stem.

If a prisoner was likely to struggle, planks were placed across the trap doors so that the warders could stand either side to restrain him. When both hangmen had stepped clear, the principal executioner pushed over the lever, and the trap doors fell, launching the prisoner to his doom. The whole operation, from entering the cell until the freeing of the trap doors, certainly took less than half-a-minute, and sometimes barely 10 seconds.

The assistant hangman and prison doctor then descended, through a small trap door, into the room below where the body was hanging. The medical officer checked for signs of life, including listening for a heart beat (which it has been claimed could continue for up to 20 minutes after the drop). Both men returned to the scaffold, which was then cleared and the room locked so the body could hang undisturbed for an hour.

At 9am, the executioners returned and, using the pulley blocks from the smaller box, lifted the corpse up, loosened the noose, and placed the body in a coffin ready to be inspected by the inquest jury. A small block of wood was placed under the dead man's head before the viewing. Apart from making their report to the governor, that effectively completed the executioners' job and they would normally have been free to leave the prison before 10am.

CHAPTER SIX

THE KILLING MACHINE

*I do not know whether a murderer is more
likely to repent and make a good end on
the gallows a few weeks after his trial or
in the prison infirmary thirty years later.*

C S Lewis

Plan and elevation of the Drop.

A plan and elevation of the trap doors, from a book by executioner James Berry. The lever, marked D, was pushed, rather than pulled as is commonly believed, forcing bar E to the left. This released the crossbars, marked O, and ensured both sections of the trap fell together. It was designed by a Royal Engineers officer in 1885.

THE MOST poignant symbol of capital punishment is the hangman's noose, and the scaffold from which it dangles. For the first half century of executions at Belfast Prison, the gallows were individually constructed for each of the prisoners, and dismantled again once the deed was done. It was a time consuming business, and other inmates of the prison were often used as unpaid labourers.

The first hangings at the prison were public affairs, with the scaffold, parts of which were borrowed from Carrick jail, erected against the prison wall but within view of the crowds which gathered in the adjoining roads and fields. While in later years every effort was made to make the prisoner's journey to the gallows as short and, hopefully, as painless as possible, little effort was made to do so in the early days. Soldier Robert Henry O'Neill, the first man to face that harrowing walk in 1854, had to make his way along the full length of D wing and up four flights of stone stairs to the "Press Room" adjacent to the gallows platform. He was spared climbing further steps on to the scaffold, and the crowd was deprived of seeing him dangling from the rope once he had fallen through the trap doors.

The arrangements for the hanging of Daniel Ward, in 1863, were very similar. However, in 1868 the law was changed, and the public were excluded from witnessing what had been a popular spectator sport. Consequently, when John Daly was sentenced to be hanged in 1876, a new location for the gallows, which took the best part of a week to construct, had to be found. The Belfast News Letter reported:

> It was placed at the entrance to what was formerly known as the debtors'
> prison, at the north end of the jail. The scaffold was in the form of an oblong
> platform, having a trap-door in the centre. This door did not, as in ordinary
> constructions of the kind, open into two parts, but opened and fell in one
> connected piece, a 56lb weight being attached to it by means of a cord, which
> passed through several small pulleys running along the lower portion of the
> platform to prevent it from springing back and coming in contact with the
> body. The platform was about 12ft wide by 16ft or 17ft long, resting on six
> strong supports, and was about 10ft from the ground. At each side were
> uprights supporting a thick cross beam, from which hung a new rope, about
> $1^1/2$ in thick, having a running noose attached.

SCALE SHOWING THE STRIKING FORCE OF FALLING BODIES AT DIFFERENT DISTANCES.

Distance Falling in Feet Zero	8 Stone	9 Stone	10 Stone	11 Stone	12 Stone	13 Stone	14 Stone	15 Stone	16 Stone	17 Stone	18 Stone	19 Stone
	Cw. Qr. lb.	Cw Qr lb.	Cw. Qr. lb.	Cw. Qr. lb.	Cw. Qr. lb.	Cw. Qr. lb.	Cw. Qr. lb.	Cw. Qr. lb.	Cw. Qr. lb.	Cw. Qr. lb.	Cw. Qr. lb.	Cw. Qr. lb.
1 Ft.	8 0 0	9 0 0	10 0 0	11 0 0	12 0 0	13 0 0	14 0 0	15 0 0	16 0 0	17 0 0	18 0 0	19 0 0
2 „	11 1 15	12 2 23	14 0 14	15 2 4	16 3 22	18 1 12	19 3 2	21 0 21	22 2 11	24 0 1	25 1 19	26 3 9
3 „	13 3 16	15 2 15	17 1 14	19 0 12	20 3 11	22 2 9	24 1 8	26 0 7	27 3 5	29 2 4	31 1 2	33 0 1
4 „	16 0 0	18 0 0	20 0 0	22 0 0	24 0 0	26 0 0	28 0 0	30 0 0	32 0 0	34 0 0	36 0 0	40 0 0
5 „	17 2 11	19 3 5	22 0 0	24 0 22	26 1 16	28 2 11	30 3 5	33 0 0	35 0 22	37 0 16	39 2 11	41 3 15
6 „	19 2 11	22 0 5	24 2 0	26 3 22	29 1 16	31 3 11	34 1 5	36 3 0	39 0 22	41 2 16	44 0 11	46 2 5
7 „	21 0 22	23 3 11	26 2 0	29 0 16	31 3 5	34 1 22	37 0 11	39 3 0	42 1 16	45 0 5	47 2 22	50 1 11
8 „	22 2 22	25 2 4	28 1 14	31 0 23	34 0 5	36 3 15	39 2 25	42 2 7	45 1 16	48 0 26	51 0 8	53 3 18
9 „	24 0 11	27 0 12	30 0 14	33 0 23	36 0 16	39 0 18	42 0 19	45 0 21	48 0 22	51 0 23	54 0 25	57 0 26
10 „	25 1 5	28 1 23	31 2 14	34 3 4	37 3 22	41 0 12	44 1 2	47 1 21	50 2 11	53 3 1	56 3 19	60 0 9

A "Table of Drops" was used by the hangmen to calculate a suitable falling distance for their victims. As a rule of thumb, they looked for a striking force of 24cwt, but could add or subtract inches according to how muscular they felt the condemned man's neck was, and allowing for his age and general health.

The passageway under the scaffold served as a viewing room, with the body lowered into a black-painted deal coffin which was then set on a stand for inspection by the inquest jury.

The one-piece trap door was an unusual contrivance even at a time when all jails designed their own scaffolds. In 1885, a former Royal Engineers' officer, Lieutenant Colonel Alten Beamish, designed for the Home Office what was to become the standard gallows. The hangman James Berry suggested a modification which called for a "slope or a level gangway" to replace steps up to the platform. This he claims was first employed in April, 1890, at Kirkdale Jail. His memory, however, let him down for as the Belfast News Letter reported of the 1889 visit of the "Bradford celebrity" to Belfast for the execution of Arthur McKeown:

> There was nothing peculiar in the scaffold, the mechanical portion was on the exact plan of all others erected in this country. There was, however, this difference taken as a whole; the culprit was not asked to ascend a staircase, the platform being on a level with the corridor.

On this occasion the scaffold was constructed at the end of D wing, next to the Mater Hospital. It was totally enclosed, with a temporary staircase also built to allow it to be entered from outside the main prison as well as through a doorway in the corridor. In order to allow a sufficient drop, a three foot trench had to be dug in the ground below the double trap doors, with the exposed clay sprinkled with sawdust. The condemned cell was now only some 30 feet away from the entrance to the gallows, a vast improvement on earlier executions. John Gilmour, hanged in 1894, died at the same spot and most likely on the same gallows, for it had become normal custom to dismantle the scaffold and store it for further use, rather than building a totally fresh one.

By the time William Woods came to breath his last in Crumlin Road Jail in 1901, however, the authorities had decided to make the scaffold a permanent fixture. The new execution chamber was in fact a stone extension of C Wing, again on the hospital side but further away from the Crumlin Road. At the time it was described as a "substantial apartment, entered from the corridor of the prison, with roughly plastered walls, and a glass roof". The trap doors themselves made up a considerable portion of the floor space. A smaller trap door in the floor lifted to reveal stairs which took the assistant executioner and doctor down into another bare room in which the body hung for an hour after the drop. These rooms, virtually unaltered, remained the place of execution within the jail up until the abolition of the death penalty.

Next to the execution chamber was the condemned cell where the prisoner and his warder escorts waited out his last days. The two rooms were connected by double doors which were opened only seconds before the execution was to take place. It must have come as a shock to many a prisoner to realise that he had been living and sleeping barely a dozen steps away from the place he was to meet his end.

The condemned cell itself was unremarkable. Essentially a normal cell, it was sparsely furnished with a bed, table and three chairs. Unusually for Crumlin Road Jail, where "slopping out" is still the norm, it was equipped with washing and toilet facilities. The prison also supplied a radio, writing paper, pens and a kettle for making tea. The last item caused some warders a wry smile. A condemned man was not allowed a belt or shoe laces, or indeed anything which could conceivably be used in a suicide attempt, yet the prison in the 1960s supplied a three-foot long kettle cable ideal for a bid to rob the hangman of his fee.

A condemned man was excluded from the normal routine of the prison. He was allowed, within reason, as many visits from friends and relatives as he liked. He was seen by the prison doctor every day while a clergyman was free to come and go as he pleased. According to the Home Office, in evidence to the Royal Commission on capital punishment in 1949, "amenities such as cards, chess, dominoes, etc, are provided in the cell, and the officers are encouraged to - and in fact invariably do - join the prisoner in these games". Newspapers and books were also provided, while "a pint of beer or stout is supplied daily on request, and 10 cigarettes or half an ounce of pipe tobacco are allowed unless there are medical reasons to the contrary". The only "medical reasons," presumably,

Confidential.

[By order of the Secretary of State, this document is to be treated as most strictly confidential, and, in any case, when a copy is supplied to a Sheriff he is requested to return it to the Prison Governor from whom he received it.]

Memorandum of Instructions for carrying out the details of an Execution.

1. The apparatus for the execution may be tested in the following manner :—

The working of the scaffold should be first tested without any weight. Then a bag of sand of the same weight as the culprit should be attached to the rope, and so adjusted as to allow the bag a drop equal to, or rather more than, that which the culprit shall receive, so that the rope may be stretched with a force of about 1,000 foot-pounds. The working of the apparatus under these conditions should then be tested. The bag must be of the approved pattern, with a thick and well-padded neck, so as to prevent any injury to the rope and leather. As the gutta-percha round the thimble of the execution ropes hardens in cold weather, care should be taken to have it warmed and manipulated immediately before the bag is tested.

2. After the completion of this testing the scaffold and all appliances should be locked up, and the key kept by the Governor or other responsible officer until the morning of the execution ; but the bag of sand should remain suspended all the night preceding the execution, so as to take the stretch out of the rope.

3. The executioner and any persons appointed to assist in the operation should make themselves thoroughly acquainted with the working of the apparatus.

4. The lever should be fixed so as to prevent any accident while the preliminary details are being carried out.

5. Death by hanging ought to result from dislocation of the neck. The length of the drop is determined according to the weight of the culprit.

6. The required length of drop is regulated as follows :—

At the end of the rope which forms the noose the executioner should see that 13 inches from the centre of the ring are marked off by a line painted round the rope ; this is to be a fixed quantity, which, with the stretching of this portion of the rope, and the lengthening of the neck and body of the culprit, will represent the average depth of the head and circumference of the neck after constriction.

About two hours before the execution the bag of sand should be raised out of the pit, and be allowed another drop so as to completely stretch the rope. Then while the bag of sand is still suspended, the executioner should measure off from the painted line on the rope the required length of drop, and should make a chalk mark on the rope at the end of this length. A piece of copper wire fastened to the chain should now be stretched down the rope till it reaches the chalk mark, and should be cut off there so that the cut end of the copper wire shall terminate at the upper end of the measured length of drop. The bag of sand should be then raised from the pit, and disconnected from the rope. The chain should now be so adjusted at the bracket that the lower end of the copper wire shall reach to the same level from the floor of the scaffold as the height of the prisoner. The known height of the prisoner can be readily measured on the scaffold by a graduated rule of six feet long. When the chain has been raised to the proper height the cotter must be securely fixed through the bracket and chain. The executioner should now make a chalk mark on the floor of the scaffold, in a plumb-line with the chain, where the prisoner should stand.

These details should be carried out as soon as possible after 6 o'clock, so as to allow the rope time to regain a portion of its elasticity before the execution, and, if possible, the gutta percha on the rope should be again warmed.

x (2)18161 Pk 12 100 7,22 E & S

2

7. The copper wire should now be detached, and after allowing sufficient amount of rope for the easy adjustment of the noose, the slack of the rope should be fastened to the chain above the level of the head of the culprit with a pack-thread. The pack-thread should be just strong enough to support the rope without breaking.

8. When all the preparations are completed the scaffold should remain in charge of a responsible officer while the executioner goes to the pinioning room.

9. The pinioning apparatus should be dexterously applied in some room or place convenient to the scaffold. When the culprit is pinioned and his neck is bared he should be at once conducted to the scaffold.

10. On reaching the gallows the duty of the executioner should be as follows :—

    (1) Place the culprit *exactly* under the part of the beam to which the rope is attached.

    (2) Strap the culprit's legs tightly.

    (3) Put on the white linen cap.

    (4) Put on the rope round the neck quite tightly (with the cap between the rope and the neck), the metal eye being directed forwards, and placed in front of the angle of the lower jaw, so that with the constriction of the neck it may come underneath the chin. The noose should be kept tight by means of a stiff leather washer, or an india-rubber washer, or a wedge.

    (5) Go *quickly* to the lever and let down the trap doors.

11. The culprit should hang one hour, and then the body should be *carefully* raised from the pit. The rope should be removed from the neck, and also the straps from the body. In laying out the body for the inquest the head should be raised three inches by placing a small piece of wood under it.

December 1891.

Home Office instructions underlining how it
expected an executioner to carry out his task.
It is unlikely, given they had been trained in the
use of the apparatus before making it onto the
approved list of hangmen, that there was ever
much call to refer to it (Public Record Office).

24th March, 1933.

Dear Mr. Stephenson,

Re Harold Courtney

I beg to inform you that I have
appointed Thomas William Pierrepoint of Town End,
Clayton, Bradford, to act at the execution of
above on Friday, 7th prox., and his nephew, Albert
Pierrepoint of 41 Mill Street, Manchester, as his
Assistant.   The latter is on the official List,
and has already acted at Mountjoy and Birmingham.
They will travel via Heysham on the night of Wednesday,
5th prox., arriving in Belfast on Thursday morning,
6th prox., and will proceed immediately to the
Prison from the boat, and report to you.   After
their arrival would you kindly phone me - Portadown 138, -
and inform me of the fact.

I intend to be at the prison on Tuesday,
4th prox. to see you about the arrangements.

Yours faithfully,

Under-sheriff, Co. Armagh.

R. W. Stephenson Esq.

Governor, H. M. Prison,

Crumlin Rd.,

BELFAST.

The prison governor, who in practice bore most
of the responsiblity for the execution once the
hangmen arrived at the jail, was kept informed of
the arrangements being made by the Under
Sheriff (Public Record Office).

which would stop such a modest comfort would be the fear the cigarettes would kill the prisoner before the State had a chance to!

Under no circumstances were other inmates allowed to meet, let alone associate, with the condemned man for fear they would help him commit suicide. On a pleasant day, for example, the prisoner might request to go for a walk in the jail's garden, which was usually granted. First, however, all other inmates were either locked in their cells or in the dining area. So as to cause as little disruption as possible, most trips out were either during breakfast, lunch or evening meal times, or after lock-up. The death watch warders would ring a bell to let the other staff know the prisoner was on his way, and he would be escorted to and from his destination as quickly and directly as possible.

All meals were cooked especially for the prisoner by an officer in the prison hospital's kitchens, again for fear inmates would poison the food in order to give the condemned man what they would see as an "easy way out". As a result his meals were of a generally higher standard and any special requests were normally honoured. All food was consumed in the condemned cell.

Warders were encouraged to strike up a relationship with the prisoner in the hope it would take some of the tension out of the situation. Six prison officers made up the death watch team. They worked in pairs and followed a complicated shift pattern. It was a traumatic time for all concerned and several reportedly had to be treated for nervous conditions in the aftermath of an execution. It is doubtful if anyone involved in the process escaped emotionally unscathed.

A hanging had a sobering affect on the entire prison population. On the actual day of execution, the prisoners would be given their breakfasts in the cells, where they remained until the early afternoon and the completion of the entire process. The jail was unusually quiet, like a Sunday. Even the terrible clanging which accompanied the opening and closing of the heavy metal doors virtually ceased, as there was little movement within the prison. As the hour of execution approached, both the silence and tension intensified. On the stroke of eight o'clock, however, the jail erupted as inmates demonstrated their anger and disgust at what was going on in their midst by banging chamber pots, metal cups and plates on floors and cell doors. After three or four minutes, the jail again lapsed into an uneasy silence.

CORONER'S COURT

City of Belfast. TO WIT.

An Inquisition indented, taken for our Sovereign Lord the King, at *His Majesty's Prison* in the City of Belfast, and in the County of *the City of Belfast* on *Friday* the *7th* day of *April* in the year of our Lord One Thousand Nine Hundred and *thirty three* and the *British Dominion beyond the Seas* in the *twenty third* year of the Reign of our Sovereign Lord GEORGE V., by the Grace of God, of the United Kingdom of Great Britain and Ireland, King, Defender of the Faith, before me, JAMES GRAHAM Medical Doctor, Coroner of our said Sovereign Lord the King for the said City of Belfast, on view of the body of *Harold Courtney* then and there lying dead,

to inquire for our said Sovereign Lord the King, when, how, and by what means the said *Harold Courtney* came to *his* death, and say

That the Said *Harold Courtney being a male person of the age of 23 years and a Motor Lorry Driver was a prisoner in the said Prison, under judgment of death, for the murder of one Minnie Reid, and that judgment of death was duly executed on him by being hanged by the neck until dead, in that the walls of the said Prison, on the day and year aforesaid, not more than twenty four hours above the holding of this Inquest, and that at the body on which this Inquest is held, is the identical Body of the said Harold Courtney adjudged to death as aforesaid.*

In Witness whereof, well as the said Coroner has hereunto set and subscribed his hand the day and year first above WRITTEN.

William Graham _____ Coroner for the said City of Belfast.

Following the abandonment of public executions, legislation required an inquest to be held within the jail so a verdict of lawful killing could be recorded. This normally sat at 10am in the governor's office and was generally, though not always, a formality. Before the sitting, the inquest jury was offered the opportunity to view the body. Officials giving evidence were urged to be as vague as possible in answering questions put to them. Indeed, in January 1925 the Home Office advised:

> *Any reference to the manner in which an execution has been carried out should be confined to as few words as possible, eg, "It was carried out expeditiously and without a hitch". No record should be taken as to the number of seconds, and, if pressed for details of this kind, the Governor should say he cannot give them as he did not time the proceedings, but "a very short interval elapsed" or some general expression of opinion to the same effect.*

Governors were, however, permitted to own up to any undue delay or hitch and give a full account of the problem.

All that remained to be done was the burial, with the grave already having been dug the previous day by the jail's trade staff. A prison chaplain conducted the funeral service, which was generally attended by the governor and warders. In the early days of the jail's history, the coffin would have been filled with quicklime to accelerate decomposition. This practice was later abandoned. Officially the graves were to be unmarked, though their exact positions are plotted on prison records. However, notches and in some cases sets of initials on the garden wall indicate where individuals are buried. Others can only be guessed at. To make it more difficult to mark the burial site, the trade staff fenced off the area around a grave until the grass had a chance to recover.

A coroner's court, sitting within the prison, went though the formalities of confirming the executed man was the same person named on the warrant and had been duly hanged as the law required (Public Record Office)

SECTION TWO

A CHRONOLOGICAL ACCOUNT

CHAPTER SEVEN

PUBLIC ENTERTAINMENT

*O Let me ask you what shall become of you
or I if we sleep the sleep of death.*

Daniel Ward
(Written while awaiting execution)

Robert Henry O'Neill spent his teenage years
living with an uncle in Hercules Street, seen here
being demolished in 1879 as part of the
redevelopment which produced Royal Avenue
(Ulster Museum).

Execution of Robert Henry O'Neill
21st June, 1854

PRIVATE Robert Henry O'Neill holds the distinction of being the first prisoner of Crumlin Road jail to have been executed. His crime was the shooting dead of Robert Brown, his corporal, on 22th August, 1853. There is some doubt as to whether the killing was a deliberate act. The events of the previous three days, however, probably swayed the jury more than anything else, for they provided a motive.

Although described by some as a sectarian crime, it seems more likely that O'Neill, a Roman Catholic, was a victim of military bullying who simply "snapped". Born in a public house in Berry Street, he had a hard upbringing. Abandoned by his mother while still an infant, O'Neill and his sister were more or less left to their own devices by their father, who died while they were still young. At the age of 13 he went to live with an uncle in Hercules Street (later to be redeveloped into Royal Avenue) but it was not a happy home. In April, 1853, at the age of 19, he enlisted in the army but almost immediately regretted it and went into hiding. Two months later he was turned in by another youth and forced to move to the barracks where, no doubt, his reception would not have been a warm one.

The unfortunate sequence of events which were to lead him to the gallows began on Saturday, 20th August, 1853, when Corporal Brown, a Londoner, ordered O'Neill and another soldier to clean windows at the barracks - a task he failed to do. The same order was given the following day, at which point the corporal told O'Neill he intended reporting him to his officer. That resulted in the private being given three days' confinement to barracks and extra drill, beginning on the Monday. During that day the discontented soldier let several of his colleagues know of his anger towards the corporal and even, it was later alleged, threatened to kill him. At 8.30pm he returned to his billet after the punishment drill, placing his musket in the rack. The corporal was already in the room, warming himself by the fire. A short time later the NCO sat himself down at a table and began writing a letter, while the other soldiers in the room lay on their beds reading or chatting. O'Neill returned to the rack and lifted down the musket and began cleaning it with a rag. A minute later the room reverberated to the crack of the firearm and the corporal lay across the table fatally wounded. He was carried to the hospital where he died two hours later. Corporal Brown was just one day short of his 20th birthday. A postmortem later revealed that the ball had struck the corporal between the eyes, passed out the left cheek, and into his chest about two inches below the collar bone, ending up in the left side of his back. O'Neill, who had thrown down the weapon and tried to make a run for it, was caught in the parade ground and placed in the guardroom.

At his trial during the Spring Assizes of March, 1854, it transpired that O'Neill had borrowed the weapon from another soldier, who had been admitted to hospital, less than three hours before the shooting. It was argued in his defence that he had been unaware the musket was loaded.

Before a packed courthouse, which included many soldiers from the 12th Regiment to which both the victim and the accused belonged, the defence argued with some justification that there was a conspiracy against O'Neill. Sergeant John Hardy, in particular, was accused of lying about an alleged confession by the prisoner on the morning following the shooting. He had not reported the guardroom incident until just four days before the trial began. The defence also asserted that, judging from the direction the ball entered the corporal's body, it must have ricocheted off a shelf first. That, they said, proved there had been no intention to harm anyone.

The jury, however, were unconvinced and returned a guilty verdict, causing the judge, Mr Sergeant Howley, to burst into tears! Sentencing was deferred until the next day when his Lordship donned the black cap, while O'Neill sobbed in the dock, to read the sentence:

> *It only remains for me to pass upon you the sentence of the law, which is that you, Robert Henry O'Neill shall be taken from the place where you now stand back to the jail, that thence, on Friday, the 5th day of May, you shall be taken to the place of common execution - the gallows - and that you shall be hanged by the neck until you be dead. Your body shall be buried within the precincts of the jail, and may the Lord have mercy on your soul.*

This time it was too much for both O'Neill and the judge. As his Lordship leaned forward, his head in his hands "under feelings of the deepest and most tender emotion," the prisoner fainted and had to be carried out of court by the warders. The drama was by no means over. Two days before the execution was due to take place, it was postponed until the 14th May to allow legal arguments to continue. News of the late, and as it turned out temporary, reprieve did not reach everyone and on the morning of 5th May crowds began gathering outside the jail to await the execution. By lunchtime there was an estimated 3,000 people and the police had to be called in to disperse them. The Banner of Ulster newspaper reported:

VICTORIA BARRACK. BELFAST. 2390. W.L.

Victoria Barracks, in North Queen Street,
had been a military base from the late eighteenth
century. The buildings to the left were built in
1883, while to the right stands the older part of
the barracks (Laurence collection,
National Library of Ireland).

*The mass of the "unwashed," unwilling to believe those who told them that
the execution would not take place, resolutely kept their ground till two
o'clock, and not a few were satisfied to occupy their positions till a late hour
in the evening. The state of feeling among the lower orders of society, indicated
by the circumstance referred to, furnishes its own melancholy comment.*

The date of execution was put back again, firstly to 22nd May, then 14th June. O'Neill
was sent to Dublin on 29th May for a hearing at the Court of Queen's Bench on 1st June,
which considered a challenge that there had been irregularities in the case regarding the
jury panel and the judge's failure to ask the prisoner if he had anything to say before
judgment was passed. Two weeks later, the court finally ruled against O'Neill and he
arrived back in Belfast on 16th June looking thinner and even more haggard than before.
He was met at the train station by a prison van which took him back to Crumlin Road
Jail, accompanied by a police escort.

O'Neill ate well on his last night despite lapsing into tearful bouts of depression. He spent time with his priests before retiring to bed, fully clothed, for several hours. At midnight he rose again and spent the rest of the night in prayer. "I will have long enough to sleep till the day of judgment," he told a prison official who encouraged him to rest longer. At 6.30am the clergy returned and Mass was said in a room adjoining the condemned cell. A brief, final visit, was allowed by an aunt and another female relative before O'Neill returned to his religious preparations.

Outside, meanwhile, police reinforcements had been drafted in, including 110 men from County Antrim and a further 30 from County Down. Even so, they were virtually overrun by the huge crowd which was rapidly gathering and who were determined that neither the law nor the heavy rain which was falling would stop them having a good time. The Banner of Ulster reported:

> Shortly after ten o'clock the brickfields, streets, roads and fields and ditches adjoining, were covered by a multitude of not less than eight thousand persons, comprising a large number of boys, principally of that class who may be seen in the Police Court hall and docks, women of disreputable appearance, and the dregs of society generally - a really respectable man not appearing within the range of our vision.

Detachments of the 62nd and 68th Foot regiments arrived at the jail shortly before 11am, and formed up inside the railings, while a troop of the Queen's Dragoon Guards forced the mob back into the fields and away from the road. At 11.30am O'Neill, dressed in army fatigues and accompanied by three priests, was led from the condemned cell in the southern wing of the prison, and up four flights of stairs into a small room off a landing. At 12.10pm he was brought out, with his hands already bound and the white cap placed on his head. As he walked on to the scaffold he came into public view for the first time and an almighty roar went up from what was now estimated as a 15,000-strong crowd. The executioner, apparently a man of considerable experience, quickly placed him on the trap door and adjusted the rope about his neck. Stepping back he pushed the lever and O'Neill disappeared from view. However, "the neck did not appear to have been broken, and a convulsive struggle continued for two minutes and a-half". The mob, no longer able to see the spectacle, fell silent. After hanging for 45 minutes, the body was taken down. In the presence of the two relatives who had earlier visited him, the corpse was stripped, dressed in a shroud and placed in a coffin to be carried to the rear of the jail for burial.

By an odd coincidence, the last person to be publicly hanged at Carrickfergus, in 1844, was also a soldier, John Cordery, who murdered his sergeant on returning to barracks after a night of heavy drinking.

The compassionate Rev William Murphy O'Hanlon, whose articles in the Northern Whig newspaper had highlighted a lack of morality among the town's poor, returned to England in October, 1854, only four months after O'Neill's execution. No doubt he would have been saddened, though not entirely surprised, by the young man's demise given his description of the barracks area:

> Let me first direct your eye to some of the purlieus of North Queen-street. Every one must have noticed the close affinity existing between intemperance and the grosser forms of sensuality; and this quarter exhibits, in immediate juxtaposition, facilities for the indulgence of both these classes of vice. How far the idle, and, in general, dissolute habits of the soldier life in barracks may have to do specially with the case, I must leave your readers to judge. But it is a fact that no region of the town seems to be more fully furnished with the elements and means of immorality than this.

Shaw's Bridge, today a haven of tranquility in
south Belfast, was the scene of a murder which
shocked the generally rural community.

Execution of Daniel Ward
8th April, 1863

SHAW'S BRIDGE, on the fringes of south Belfast, today plays host to thousands of visitors, who picnic in the adjoining car park or enjoy quiet walks along the tow path by the River Lagan. But the bridge's narrow roadway was formerly a busy thoroughfare which linked counties Antrim and Down and, in 1862, a magnet for people who wanted to see for themselves the scene of a murder which had sent ripples of disgust and shock through the townsfolk of Belfast and beyond.

It was on 10th May, 1862, that the tranquillity of what was then the heart of the countryside was shattered by the spilling of blood for the pathetic sum of just £2. The victim, Charles Wilgar, was a carpenter by trade who was working away from his Ballylesson home. During the week he would stay with an uncle, William Wright, on what is now the Upper Malone Road, going home after work on a Saturday to be with his parents, who lived some three miles away. On this particular weekend he had tea at the Wright's as usual and then set off in the company of Daniel Ward, a fellow carpenter who had called at the house earlier in the day. When Wilgar failed to arrive home his parents raised the alarm. Ward, when approached by the family, said he had left Wilgar early on, after the young man had said he was going to meet his brother returning from Belfast.

The police at Newtownbreda were called in and soon established that a watch belonging to Wilgar had been pawned in Lisburn on the same night he had disappeared. Ward, the natural suspect, his wife and mother-in-law were then arrested on suspicion and lodged in Downpatrick Jail. On Wednesday, 14th May, a search of the river bank turned up signs of a struggle and a boat was sent for. Within a few hours the river gave up Wilgar's body. Stewart McClieve, one of those who had fished it out, later recalled: "There was blood all round his head. The blood streamed from his head when he was taken out of the water." The river in the immediate vicinty was then dragged and a stone tied up in a handkerchief recovered.

When the case against Ward came to trial, the demand for seats in the County Courthouse, Belfast, was such that tickets had to be issued. A series of witnesses gave evidence that they had seen Wilgar and Ward leave the house together about 6.30pm on the Saturday and walk towards Shaw's Bridge. Others told how they had noticed the prisoner on his own a short time later, walking away from the river. Later still, Ward was seen in Lisburn, with several people placing him in the pawn shop where Wilgar's watch was found. One of the most damning pieces of evidence came not from a witness, but a second watch. This had been given to Wilgar by his uncle, just before he left the house, so he in turn could pass it on to his brother. The transaction had been completed out of Ward's sight, and the watch was still in the dead man's pocket when the body was recovered. It had stopped at a quarter past seven, giving a possible time when the body had entered the river. After a three-day hearing, the jury returned a guilty verdict and the judge, Baron Deasy, pronounced sentence of death. Visibly affected by the moment, he donned the black cap:

> *It now only remains for me to terminate the painful scene by announcing in formal terms that sentence which the law requires the judge to pronounce, and compels the executive ministers of justice to carry into effect, and that sentence is that you, Daniel Ward, be taken from the dock in which you now stand to the jail in which you have hitherto been confined, and that from that you be taken on Wednesday, the 8th day of April, to the place of public execution, and there be hanged by the neck till you are dead, and that your body be buried within the precincts of the jail within which you shall have been last confined after conviction. And may the great God who has created you have mercy upon your immortal soul.*

Ward, who had shown no emotion throughout, remained resolute. Catching his forelock with his right hand, he bowed to the bench, turned, and smartly left the dock. Throughout his trial Ward had maintained his innocence. Once found guilty, however, he immediately dropped the pretence and wrote out a full confession, which was published after his death. It left no doubt as to his guilt and spelt out clearly just how desperate a man he was:

> *I, Daniel Ward, now a prisoner in the County of Antrim Jail, Belfast, and under sentence of death for the murder of Charles Wilgar, on the 10th of May last, in the presence of Almighty God, before whom I must soon stand, do make the following confession, and declare every portion of it to be strictly true:*
>
> *On the evening of the 9th May I was in Belfast seeking for employment at any work I could obtain but did not succeed. I left Belfast between four and five o'clock that evening, and, during my walk home I thought of, as the last remedy, robbing or murdering someone in order to get money. My mind did not settle at that time on anyone in particular but I felt no act whatever would prevent me from obtaining it.*
>
> *Before reaching home, I called at William Wright's to ask him if he could give me a job, for I was idle. So far, as to murdering Charles Wilgar in particular had not taken possession of my mind, nor any other, if I could get money in any other way. On the next morning, May the 10th, I went to*

The County Antrim Jail, Crumlin Road, Belfast, about 1870. Completed in 1845, there were to be 17 executions within its walls in the next 120 years (Ulster Museum).

Belfast. On going, I sat upon a heap of stones, thinking what to do; I took up a stone, and put it into my pocket-handkerchief. I left Belfast between three and four o'clock that evening. On this evening, also. I went to William Wright's and waited till Wright and Wilgar returned from work.

My object in waiting in Wright's was till it was dusk, that I might obtain by some means what I wanted, and had not up till this time settled my mind in taking the life of Charles Wilgar. After tea in Wright's, I started, with Charles Wilgar, towards home, and I do not think it was five minutes before the act that I determined to take his watch or life. I knew he had a watch. We came to a narrow path – he went on before me. I took then the stone which was in my handkerchief out of my pocket and gave him a blow. He fell, but did not speak. He was rising, I think, on his hands and feet. I then gave him the second blow – took his watch from him, and put him into the water. The plunge appeared to revive him, for I saw him swimming across the Lagan, and thought he would get out at the other side. I then threw the stone and the handkerchief into the water, and went to Lisburn and pawned the watch for two pounds – and when, on Monday evening, I heard he was missing, I knew he was drowned.

Ward was obviously not a popular man. Indeed, a petition begging for a reprieve apparently received little support for fear it might actually succeed and result in him eventually returning to the neighbourhood. There was a widespread suspicion that he may have been involved in other violent incidents. Ward himself appears to have referred to these allegations in another part of his confession when he said: "I also solemnly declare, before God, that I never injured so as to take away the life of any other man, woman, or child."

Ward's last few days in jail were marked with the same outward composure he had displayed throughout his imprisonment and trial. Although two warders were with him constantly at nights, with another posted outside the door in case assistance was needed, only the latter precaution was considered necessary during the day. On the Monday of his last week his parents visited him, and "sobbed as if their hearts would break" as they parted. The following day his mother and an aunt came to the prison and again the tears flowed, though not on the part of Ward who, bar a momentary lapse in the presence of his Episcopalian clergyman, the Rev Charles Allen, remained steadfastly dry-eyed. His wife, however, failed to make an appearance. She had left for Scotland on the day the judgment was announced, leaving the couple's child with its grandmother.

On Wednesday, 8th April, 1863, he rose early after a fairly sound night's sleep. At 6am he was joined by the Rev Allen for almost two hours of devotion. Like many a condemned man before and after him, Ward had turned to God in his blackest hour, making his last four months "the happiest days of my life". At 7.45am, a solemn procession formed up outside the condemned cell. With Ward, cap in hand, in the centre, the clergyman to his left and a warder to the right, he began his final journey. Behind came several warders, the High Sheriff, the Under Sheriff, and the Governor of the jail walking in pairs. A posse of journalists brought up the rear. Slowly they made their way along the passageway and up the stairs, stopping in the room which led out to the scaffold. Further prayers were said before the hangman appeared some 10 minutes after eight o'clock and pinioned Ward's arms behind his back. Still accompanied by the Rev Allen and a jailor, he was led out on to the scaffold which, as in the previous execution, had been erected at the front of the jail so as to be fully visible to the public. Ward, already dressed in his shroud, remained calm throughout, and even lent his head to one side to make it easier for the executioner to attach the rope. As the hangman retreated, Ward made one last appeal to heaven: "O Lord Jesus, be merciful to my soul. God pardon my sins for the sake of the Redeemer, and bless all my fellow creatures". At this point the bolt was withdrawn and he plunged through the gap. The crowd, estimated to be up to 9,000 strong, let out a shriek, breaking the silence which had befallen it on the prisoner's appearance. Lacking a shoe, which had came off when a foot caught the edge of the drop, the body hung for about an hour before being taken down and placed in a coffin.

Only the officials who had made up the death procession were present when burial took place in a plot close to O'Neill's last resting place.

CHAPTER EIGHT

A PRIVATE AFFAIR

To prevent such frightful spectacles in a Christian country and all the incalculable evils they engender, I would have the last sentence of the law executed with comparative privacy within the prison walls.

Charles Dickens

(after witnessing a public execution)

Durham Street, where murderer John Daly lived, and the alleyways and streets off it were among the poorest in the city by the late nineteenth century. Beatty's Entry, close to where the body of Daly's victim, Margaret Whitley, was found, clearly illustrates the deprivation even some 30-odd years later when this photograph was taken (Hogg collection, Ulster Museum).

Execution of John Daly
26th April, 1876

THE RESIDENTS of Bathurst Court, a tiny row of houses off Belfast's Durham Street, awoke on the morning of 15th September, 1875, to a sight which was to chill them to the bone. Lying on the pavement was the naked body of a woman, her corpse a bloodied mess. A crowd soon gathered to gawp, but no one was able to put a name to the poor unfortunate. Eventually a little girl, drawn to the court by all the commotion, identified the victim as a charwoman called Margaret Whitley, who had lived close by. The search for her killer could now start in earnest, and it wasn't long before a picture started to emerge. Within hours it had been established that the dead woman was a relative of the wife of a coal porter named John Daly, who lived in Durham Street. It was also soon learnt that she had spent the previous evening at the Daly household and that there had been some sort of fracas. Daly was arrested as he went about his work and his house searched. Before the day was out the police had gathered enough evidence to guarantee Daly an appointment with the hangman.

John Daly, 47 at the time of his execution, was born to a farming family who worked a smallholding close to Dungannon. One of three children, he lost his father while still very young. His older brother was also to lose his life tragically early in an accident at a local coalpit. Daly took on the responsibility for the running of the farm and managed to support the rest of the family. However, a dispute over the land led to a family rift, and Daly left the farm and headed for Belfast in 1863. He found work labouring on the quayside and soon fell in with a mill girl named Mary Anne Whitley, a niece of the murdered woman. It was she, and the demon drink, which were to be the cause of his downfall.

Both Daly and his wife became alcoholics, living in squalor to afford their habit. Their two rooms in the house in Durham Street, which they shared with their 12-year-old daughter and blind infant son, were virtually devoid of furnishings. The bed was a pile of straw spread on the floor and covered with a cloth. A table and stool were the only other pieces of furniture. Everything else which had once adorned the house had been pawned for cash for drink, principally by Mrs Daly who frequently indulged her addiction with her maiden aunt, Margaret Whitley, also an alcoholic. This, it would appear, rankled with Daly.

On the Monday before the murder, in what was probably not an untypical occurrence, a row had erupted in the Daly home which resulted in him throwing his wife out. The following day he arrived home from work early to find she had returned to the house and once again he turned on her, this time using violence to force her out. Daly then gave his daughter the family clock to pawn before heading back to work. However, the cash was spent by Mrs Daly and Whitley on alcohol - no doubt the purpose Daly had had in mind for himself - and when he arrived home he found both of them drunk in the house. His wife, however, was not so intoxicated that she did not realise the danger and fled on seeing him, leaving her aunt lying on the makeshift bed. Daly, outraged, picked up the stool and struck the woman in the presence of his daughter, who then fled the house. Unperturbed, Daly continued his savage attack, inflicting wounds to the head, face, arms and abdomen.

When the frenzy passed, he realised he would have to dispose of the body. Just how he managed that is a matter for conjecture, for Daly never confessed to the murder. It would appear that, in order to avoid leaving a trail of blood, he had first stripped away the bloodied garments then wrapped the corpse in items of clothing belonging to his wife. Then, sometime during the night, he attached a rope to the body and dragged it from his house to the spot where it was found. Possibly using the same method and rope, which was later found by the police in the house, he dragged her clothes to a drain a little distance away. Daly then set off for his work as usual. Later, when he was arrested, the police checked for blood stains on his body, but could find none. A search of the house, however, provided ample evidence of violence. The bed and walls were liberally splattered with blood, while the floor "seemed as if blood had been actually spilled out of a vessel on it".

The two-day trial could only have one conclusion and Daly became the next resident of Crumlin Road Jail's condemned cell. He threw himself into the spiritual preparations for his death. ably aided by the Roman Catholic chaplain and the Sisters of Mercy. But though on the eve of his death he was to praise both the Governor and his warders for their care and attention, he virtually refused to speak with them throughout his imprisonment. On the Monday before the execution his mother paid him a last emotional visit during which both parties wept openly. The meeting was ended early, with the Governor promising she could return the next day. Later still, Daly's wife, who according to the Belfast News Letter had "by her want of prudence and propriety hastened the degradation and ruin of her husband" called with him. She was the last relative to see him, for Daly sent a message to his mother asking her to go home to Dungannon and not remain in Belfast for the execution.

Meanwhile, the finishing touches to the scaffold were being completed. Since Ward's hanging, the law had been altered and executions were no longer to take place in public. As a consequence, the gallows were built at the north end of the jail, outside what had once been known as the debtors' prison.

On Tuesday, his last night, clergy and two Sisters of Mercy joined him for his religious devotions. After a few hours sleep, he was awakened by a warder at 5.30am and celebrated

Mass in his cell at 6am. Two hours later, at the appointed time, the executioner entered the cell and pinioned his arms, after the Sub Sheriff had read the execution warrant in the presence of the prison Governor. The formalities completed, Daly, dressed in prison clothing and physically shaking with fear, began the short walk to the scaffold. Alongside him, reading prayers, was the priest, with the executioner behind. Once at the gallows, it was all over in seconds, the hangman swiftly adjusting the white cap and rope before stepping back to release the trap door. The drop of approximately eight feet was apparently sufficient to cause instant death.

Outside the jail a considerable crowd had gathered, filling the Crumlin Road and spilling into its side streets. Many were on their way to work and had taken time out to be there at the critical moment. Others hung out of the upstairs windows of the houses opposite the jail in the hope of catching sight of the condemned man. There was, of course, little for them to see, though by standing on tiptoe at one part of the road it was just possible to see the very top of the scaffold. A few minutes before 8am, the prison bell began to toll its dismal message that all was prepared. Then a few minutes past the hour, the black flag was hoisted, signalling that Daly was dead.

By the time the body was taken down, at 9am, the crowd had dispersed and all had returned to normal in the outside world. The corpse was lowered into a black-painted plain deal coffin and placed under the scaffold. At 12.30pm, the inquest jury gathered in the jail's boardroom and its members were led down to the gallows to view the body, which "bore no evidence of contortion; the mouth was partially open, and on the neck beneath the chin was a slight mark where the rope had encircled it". The jury found, as in all cases, that the executed man had been lawfully hanged. Shortly after the inquest concluded, Daly's body was stripped of clothing and the coffin filled to the brim with quicklime to aid decomposition. The lid was screwed down and the coffin lowered into an unmarked grave alongside the previous two victims of the gallows.

It had been the Capital Punishment Amendment Act of 1868 which had brought an end to the spectacle of hanging people in front of a howling crowd. The last public execution in Britain was that of Michael Barrett, who was hanged at Newgate Prison by William Calcraft on 26th May, 1868. Barrett had been convicted for his part in an attempt by the Fenians to release Irish prisoners by blasting them out of Clerkenwell House of Detention in London. Twelve people died in the explosion, which demolished part of a wall.

Daly's execution was the fourth in Ulster since the reforms. The others had been at Downpatrick, Cavan and Omagh. The last of these involved the infamous Thomas Hartley Montgomery, a police officer who hacked a Northern Bank cashier to death during a robbery. He underwent three trials before a verdict of guilty was delivered, after which he faked insanity in a last desperate bid to escape the gallows. He was hanged at Omagh jail in August, 1873.

The infamous Thomas Hartley Montgomery,
executed in Omagh jail in August, 1873, was one
of the first men in Ulster to be hanged out of the
public gaze. A serving RIC officer, his three trials
and ultimate conviction for the murder of a
Northern Bank cashier in Newtownstewart –
whom he beat to death with a billhook to steal
£1,605 – caused a sensation in its day.

Execution of Arthur McKeown
14th January, 1889

MURDER is not a crime of the criminal classes but of amateurs, the Royal Commission of 1949-53 concluded. It was fair comment. While a handful of executions carried out at Crumlin Road jail followed killings perpetrated during robberies, only one was committed by a truly professional criminal. The remainder were strictly amateurs, or at worst, petty crooks, whose ham-fisted attempts almost inevitably ended in a trip to the gallows. The majority, however, were the results of domestic circumstances, where the only crime committed was the actual murder itself. Such was the case of the next man to have his neck broken at the end of a rope in the County Jail.

Arthur McKeown savagely beat to death his common-law wife for refusing to leave her lover to attend a sick child. It was what the newspapers of the day would have termed a "melancholy drama". Described as an "ardent Fenian," McKeown was a man of strong political sentiments. As a teenager he had headed a procession to Hannahstown on 15th August, riding a white horse and dressed as Robert Emmet – who ironically also ended his days on the scaffold. That parade, like the 1803 Rebellion, ended in chaos when it was attacked by Protestants. The marchers retreated to Millfield where they were hemmed in for several hours.

McKeown married as a young man, but the relationship failed. In time he took up with Mary Jane Phillips, who bore him two sons. It was not a match made in heaven. She was a drunkard who periodically went off with lovers. He also drank too much and regularly resorted to violence. The couple's neighbours in Belfast's Robert Street, off Academy Street, were continually disturbed by vicious rows, at least one of which resulted in McKeown landing in prison for a time.

In July 1888, Mary Jane left him and went to live with another man. McKeown, who described himself as a car driver although he had been without work for a considerable time, took charge of the children for whom he genuinely cared. Nonetheless, having been abandoned obviously angered him and when one of the youngsters fell ill he decided it was time Mary Jane came home. On 25th August, 1888, he went looking for her at the home of Anne McCabe in Morrow's Entry, off Hill Street, arriving shortly before 10.30pm. He insisted on searching the house, forcing Mrs McCabe to strike a match so he could peer through the darkness of the upstairs bedrooms, but without joy. Infuriated, he turned to the woman and told her: "Well, Mrs McCabe, you have done that neat to get her out of the way, but once I get her I'll put her that she will not run away – I'll put an end to her."

In fact, Mary Jane was hiding in the kitchen of the house and chose that moment, when she looked to have got away with it, to rush out of the room to meet McKeown with the words: "Arthur, I'm here, I am yours and you are mine." The fine sentiments failed to wash with McKeown, who grabbed her by the throat, forcing her down on to a seat, and demanding she come home. When she refused he struck her the first of five blows with his clenched fist, each drawing blood with the help of a ring he wore. "It is hard to go home to be killed," Mary Jane reportedly told him at one stage. McKeown eventually dragged her out into the street, pulling her along until she conceded and began walking alongside him.

Less than two hours later, at 12.15am, McKeown was spotted in Robert Street standing opposite his own house by Margaret Crommie, a neighbour who sometimes helped look after the children. She called over to him and he told her Mary Jane was either dead or dying. She, in turn, summoned a police patrol which was by chance passing along the street, and the officers found the woman's body lying on the floor in a pool of blood. According to a police account, an effort had been made to clean up some of the mess. A short distance away was a bed on which the youngest of the couple's children, a boy of six, lay sleeping. McKeown, apparently without prompting, then launched into an account of the evening, which was noted down by an officer and read to the court at the Ulster Winter Assizes held in the County Courthouse, Crumlin Road, in December that year:

> You need not be uneasy about her, she has often been this way before. All the woman wants is to get pumped, then she will be all right. The fact of the matter is she has me robbed. She went away in July last, taking £7 or £8 with her and when she got me away at the Maze races she took two or three more out of that chest of drawers. Tonight I got her in a house in Morrow's Entry, and brought her home. Shortly afterwards we went to bed. I was lying at the wall, and she next the floor. About eleven o'clock the children awakened me, saying their mother was at the drawer again. When I got up she was lying as you see her. I then rose and went out and told Maggie Crommie. She said it would be better to tell the police. There was a bottle of whisky on the drawer when we went to bed, and if you were to see all that's left of it. I suppose she was drunk and fell out of bed. Do you accuse me of giving her foul play?

How the Belfast News Letter, which put out a special edition on the morning of McKeown's execution, reported the Robert Street murderer's demise.

THE

ROBERT STREET MURDER.

EXECUTION

OF

ARTHUR M'KEOWN.

THE SCENE ON THE SCAFFOLD.

THE INQUEST.

SKETCH OF THE FELON'S LIFE.

YESTERDAY morning, at the statutory hour of eight o'clock, Arthur M'Keown, convicted of the murder of Mary Jane Phillips in August last, paid the full penalty of his offence on the scaffold. The morning was unusually fine; there was a slight frost in the air, and the accompanying haze or fog delayed the coming daylight. It was not the morning for the dread work that was about to be done inside the walls of the county prison. As early as seven o'clock, just as the lamps were being turned out, the public were astir, and as they wended their way towards the jail gates, there was a manifest feeling of curiosity exhibited on each countenance as to the companionships that were being formed. From Carlisle Circus, up to the grey, dull walls inside of which the unfortunate man was confined, knots of men and women blocked the footpaths, discussing the sensationalism of the hour. They were chiefly of that class in whose favour times never change, and with which the world still wages war. As the minutes rolled past, the crowds increased, and as the sun had now substituted the stars, a quarter round the eager throng indicated the quarters from which the majority of them were drawn. Nothing worse, however, marked their conduct than the pleasantries peculiar to waiting, and the forty members of the Royal Irish Constabulary, under District-Inspector M'Ardle, sheltered in the hall of the Courthouse opposite, were not called upon to interfere. Twenty minutes before eight, five uncomfortable-looking members of the local Press presented themselves at the entrance gates to the prison, and after a preliminary process of self-identification, and a subsequent roll-call on the part of the admitting official, they were placed in charge of the head warder, Mr. Coulter. The first move was to examine the scaf-

executioner indicated that the preliminary stage had been disposed of, and proceeding through a door to the right the felon was for the first time brought within view of the scaffold. The same downcast, dejected, miserable appearance remained, and, as far as could be observed, he never lifted his eyes nor exhibited the least concern while thus walking to his doom. Berry now directed his progress, and, pointing out his position on the drop, it was assumed without apparent emotion. The final act was a short one. The white cap was produced, and placed over his eyes, the legs were strapped, the assistant handed the executioner the noose, which he adjusted with magical dexterity, and stepping aside he touched the lever, and Arthur M'Keown was launched into eternity. Just before the bolt was drawn he prayed in a loud voice, "Lord Jesus receive my soul," "Into Thy hands, O Lord, I commend my spirit," the three last words of which he had barely uttered ere his lips were sealed for ever. There was no "dull thud," as often marks an execution, the opening of the drop and the slight rattling of the rope were the only sounds audible to those at a distance of only three or four yards. Passing down below Dr. Stewart was already there, watch in hand, watching the indications that presented themselves in the features and body of the unfortunate M'Keown. After an interval of half a minute, there were two or three sharp twitches on the left cheek and eye, visible by the uplifting of the white cloth, but beyond this there was no evidence of life. Berry assured all present that death was instantaneous, and that the execution was one of the most successful he had ever conducted. After a few minutes the straps were removed from the legs and arms, and the white cap being pulled aside, showed the face to be somewhat livid, the eyes half closed, and the tongue slightly protruding—in reality, a sickening spectacle. It may be added that the unfortunate man, since the refusal of the prayers of the memorials, has attended with marked devotion to the ministrations of the prison chaplain, and was quite resigned to his fate. He did not retire to rest till two o'clock yesterday morning, and after having a broken sleep for three hours, he arose at five o'clock. The chaplain was again in attendance at six, and celebrated mass and the holy communion. The culprit, when asked, refused to partake of any breakfast, and he died without making any formal confession of his guilt. The black flag was hoisted just on the stroke of eight o'clock, and the large crowds having their morbid curiosity satisfied, quietly dispersed. With reference to our "stop-press" edition issued yesterday morning, we may state that the *Belfast News-Letter* containing the full facts of the execution, as witnessed by our special representative, was on sale on the streets of the city at twenty minutes to nine o'clock. This was the only account by an eye-witness, and written actually *after* the occurrence, which was available until considerably after that hour. It is but fair to add that the prison arrangements were all that could be desired. The Press are under deep obligations to the Under-Sheriff for his extreme courtesy, and also to Mr. M'Kenna, the deputy-governor of the jail, for the interest he took in giving them all the facilities at his disposal for the performance of what to them was anything but a pleasing duty.

THE INQUEST.

At nine o'clock the body was cut down, and at a quarter-past twelve o'clock the Coroner (Dr. Dill) held an inquest on the remains in the Boardroom of the County Jail.

Mr. Hugh M'Neile M'Cormick, Clerk of the Crown; Mr. Henry Haigh Bottomley, Sub-Sheriff for the County of Antrim; Mr. Jeremiah M'Kenna, Deputy-Governor of the jail; and District-Inspector M'Ardle were in attendance.

The following gentlemen were sworn upon the jury:—Messrs. John Trainor, publican, Old Lodge Road; Thomas Conroy, civil bill officer, 13, Ponsonby Avenue; Robert Dick, pensioner, Woodland Avenue; Robert Wilson, T.C., contractor, 8, Cavendish Terrace; Henry Scott, druggist, Eliza Street; Patrick Quigley, spirit merchant, 18, Hillman Street; Adam Turner, auctioneer, Clifton Street; William Moore, traveller, Lincoln Avenue; Patrick Leonard, hotelkeeper, Duncairn Arms; John Corkorin, R.I.C., pensioner; John M'Auley, lamplighter, 4, Ashton Street;

M'Keown was tried, convicted, and sentenced to be hanged on January 14th. This morning, at eight o'clock, I saw that warrant carried out. In pursuance of the warrant I attended at the County Antrim Jail, and formally demanded the body of Arthur M'Keown from the Deputy-Governor. This having been done, I handed the condemned man over to James Berry, public executioner, who carried out the sentence in my presence. That sentence was that he should be hanged by the neck until he was dead. I waited until the doctor stated that he was dead, and in about an hour after I saw the body cut down. I was in court during the trial. I heard the verdict of guilty returned by a jury of the County of Antrim, and heard the sentence of death pronounced by the Right Honourable Mr. Justice Holmes.

Mr. ROBERT WILSON—I suppose you don't know where Berry is now?

Witness—I do not.

Mr. WILSON—When did you last see him?

Witness—I think it was about a quarter-past nine o'clock. He asked me if he could go away, and I said he could, as I did not want him any longer.

Mr. LEONARD—Do the implements with which the execution was carried out belong to him?

Witness—Yes, the rope and pinioning straps are his.

Mr. WILSON—Was it a rope or a chain that went round the man's neck?

Witness—It was a rope, of course.

Mr. LEONARD—Don't you think it would be more satisfactory for the jurors if they could have an opportunity of seeing the rope or other appliances with which death was caused?

Witness—I don't see that it would.

Mr. LEONARD—I think that in a case of this kind we should have the evidence of the executioner, and should also see the rope with which a man's life is taken away. I think it would be more satisfactory.

Witness—I do not agree with you at all, but, of course, I shall not discuss the matter.

Mr. RANKIN—I think that the proper thing would be that the executioner should be detained until after the inquest for the purpose of giving evidence as to how the sentence was carried out. He alone can give that evidence.

Mr. LEONARD—Is it necessary that we should have his evidence.

Witness—The coroner will direct you as to whether the evidence is sufficient or not, but, in my opinion, no good object could be secured by the production of the executioner.

CORONER—Gentlemen, we will have the medical evidence, and that must be your guide in finding out the cause of death. Neither of the gentlemen that we have had produced, not even the executioner if he were here, could give you authoritative evidence as to the cause of death. That evidence must come from the doctor, and we will have it now. Of course, what the juror has just said is perfectly right, as an expression of opinion, as any juror has a right to express his opinion upon this or any other matter connected with the inquiry, but I must tell you that the only authority in law for the cause of death is the medical testimony, which we will hear in a moment or two.

Witness—I may tell you that Berry stated that, although he has carried out many executions, he has never yet been required to attend and give evidence before a jury.

CORONER—There is no statute law upon the subject, but precedent and custom have fixed it, and never within my memory had the public executioner been present or given evidence before a jury. That is the custom.

Mr. LEONARD—But it is not too late to change that custom, and in the opinion of myself and others of the jury the executioner should be present to give evidence.

Mr. SHIELDS—As a juror, and I would ask the representatives of the Press to take a note of it. I protest against this practice of smuggling the hangman out by the back door after an execution.

Witness—I think such a statement is unwarrantable, and should not be made.

CORONER—Now, gentlemen, under the law, as it stands at present, these executions are carried out in private, and, I think, most properly so, in the interests of public decency; but although the execution is private, this inquiry is quite public, and with that view, I left instructions that no person having any interest whatever in the inquiry should be excluded from it.

Mr. WILSON—Consequently, we should have all the evidence before us.

CORONER—You will have all that is necessary or available. We will now take the evidence of the medical officer of the jail.

John Stewart stated—I am medical officer of her Majesty's Prison of Belfast, and I was present at

The police did, indeed, think he had given her "foul play" and charged him a few hours later. The jury agreed, particularly after hearing the catalogue of injuries uncovered by the doctors who carried out a postmortem on Mary Jane's body two days after the killing. These included eight broken ribs, a ruptured small intestine and severe bruising to the chest and abdomen, swelling around the left eye and cuts about the right, a bruised lower lip, a cut on the chin which went to the bone, a two-inch wound to the jaw, lacerations and bruising to the left cheek, and damage to the nose. A loss of blood caused by the severing of the aorta was cited as being the main cause of death. After only 30-minutes deliberation on the part of the jurors, McKeown was found guilty and sentenced to death. He was lodged in the condemned cell just 10 days before Christmas.

Every effort was made to make McKeown, evidently dejected by his situation, as comfortable as possible. A fire was lit in the cell's hearth and the prison medical officer did his bit to warm the inner man by prescribing an ounce of brandy for the prisoner every three hours for the first 30 hours after sentencing. This was reduced to two bottles of stout and three ounces of whiskey every day up until the Lord Lieutenant turned down a plea for mercy, when it was raised to five ounces of whiskey plus the bottles of stout. McKeown was also entitled to half an ounce of tobacco per day.

Even so, no amount of drink could drown out the knowledge of his impending doom. His last night, apart from about three hours tossing and turning in bed, was spent pacing the floor. At 5am he gave up all thought of sleep and prepared instead to meet his God, celebrating Mass with a priest an hour later. He refused breakfast, and the opportunity to confess his guilt. A few moments after 8am, on 14th January, 1889, the solemn procession consisting of the Under Sheriff of County Antrim, the deputy governor, the prison doctor, two clergymen, McKeown and several warders, arrived at the scaffold. As they had come along the passageway, the prisoner could be heard joining in the responses to the prayers for the dying being recited by the priest, whose voice faltered at times as he struggled to restrain his own emotions. Within three or four yards of the end of the corridor, executioner James Berry stepped forward and pinioned McKeown's arms. A Belfast News Letter reporter, whose account appeared in a special edition of the newspaper published within three-quarters of an hour of the trap doors falling, takes up the story:

> *A sign from the executioner indicated that the preliminary stage had been disposed of, and proceeding through a door to the right the felon was for the first time brought within view of the scaffold. The same downcast, dejected, miserable appearance remained, and, as far as could be observed, he never lifted his eyes nor exhibited the least concern while thus walking to his doom. Berry now directed his progress, and pointing out his position on the drop, it was assumed without apparent emotion. The final act was a short one. The white cap was produced, and placed over his eyes, the legs were strapped, the assistant handed the executioner the noose, which he adjusted with magical dexterity, and stepping aside he touched the lever, and Arthur McKeown was*

launched into eternity. Just before the bolt was drawn he prayed in a loud voice, "Lord Jesus receive my soul, into Thy Hands, O Lord, I commend my spirit," the three last words of which he had barely uttered ere his lips were sealed for ever. There was no 'dull thud' as often marks an execution, the opening of the drop and the slight rattling of the rope were the only sounds audible to those at a distance of only three or four yards.

Within seconds the prison doctor, watch in hand, was examining the body for signs of life. The heart was still beating and McKeown's left cheek and eye twitched several times, but nonetheless life was declared to be extinct. A few minutes later the straps binding the arms and feet were removed and the white cap pulled aside to show the face to be "somewhat livid, the eyes half closed, and the tongue slightly protruding – in reality, a sickening spectacle".

An inquest opened in the prison boardroom at 12.15pm, with the jurors, once sworn in, being conducted by the deputy governor to the end of the passage where McKeown's body lay in the traditional plain wood coffin. The lid was removed by a warder and each member of the jury viewed the corpse in turn. They returned to the boardroom in a hostile mood and demanded to know why Berry had not remained in the prison to be quizzed about the execution. They then asked to see the rope used, but were again to be disappointed as the hangman had taken it with him. Finally they complained about a swelling around McKeown's eye, which had been clearly visible at the viewing. At long last, however, it was agreed that the execution had been a lawful killing and McKeown took his place in an unmarked grave to the rear of the prison.

Lyle Gardner's remains lie in a churchyard at Derrykeighan, a couple of miles outside Dervock. The head stone, erected in 1932 to his son's memory, makes no mention of the circumstances of his father's death.

Execution of John Gilmour
17th August, 1894

AS LYLE GARDNER stood in front of his kitchen fire undressing for bed, on 30th April, 1894, he must have wondered just what had happened to his snug existence of barely a week before. His only daughter, Jane, had given birth to an illegitimate child eight days previously and now relationships between himself and the Gilmour family next door were strained after the girl had claimed their son, John, was the baby's father. Indeed, less than half-an-hour earlier that evening, Gardner and his wife had had an argument with the young man on their own doorstep, with the allegations flying thick and fast. The incident was still troubling the old man as he prepared to retire for the night. The rest of the household, consisting of his daughter and new grandchild, Gardner's infant son William, and servant boy John Rodgers, were already in bed. Only he and his wife, who was busy raking out the ashes from the fire, remained downstairs as the kitchen clock ticked towards nine o'clock. Suddenly a shot rang out, the retort coming from a gun discharged through a window, and Gardner fell wounded. His wife managed to catch hold of him, saving the old man from crashing to the floor. She screamed for help and managed to raise Jane, who helped her pull Gardner on to the bed. Dr Peter Camac was sent for, and he in turn called for the assistance of Dr Robert Craig, but Gardner lost his battle for life before the second medic arrived, and less than an hour after being shot. A postmortem showed he had been hit by more than 40 pellets, mostly in the abdomen.

A man of 78, and twice married, Gardner had been an active member of his community. He had spent what turned out to be his last day working a pair of horses on his smallholding at Ballyhevistock, a few miles outside the village of Dervock, in north Antrim. The Gilmours' farmhouse stood just across the way, little more than 600 yards separating the front doors. Relationships between the families, up until the birth of the child on 22nd April, had been extremely good. However, the possibility of a lawsuit to establish 21-year-old John Gilmour as the father of Jane's child, and so force him to pay maintenance, had understandably cast a shadow over the friendship. Under law, Jane herself could not take any action against Gilmour, but Gardner, as her father, could instigate court proceedings for the wrong done to his daughter. That, it was later argued, was the sole motive for the farmer's murder.

The birth of the child had come as a complete shock to Gardner and his wife for Jane, by starving herself to compensate for her developing bulge, had managed to conceal her pregnancy from them right up until she went into labour. Gilmour, on the other hand, had been told by Jane some six months previously that she was expecting his child, but had turned his back on her. But once the baby was born, and the allegation made that he had fathered it, Gilmour could no longer simply turn a blind eye. Instead he cooked up a clumsy, poorly thought through plan to kill the old man and so, he thought, save the embarrassment and shame of a court case.

On the afternoon of the murder, about 3pm, Gilmour set off with a horse to Dervock, less than three miles away, and left it at the village blacksmith's to be shod. He then travelled on to Ballymoney, in a cart hired from McCann's and driven by one of their employees, David McBride. The two separated on arrival, with Gilmour heading for Hamill's shop, which stocked a wide range of goods. There he bought a "cheap fowling piece" for £2, some powder and shot, as well as other odds and ends. Gilmour, who made the unusual request to have the gun wrapped in brown paper, returned to the shop later to collect the weapon just before heading back to Dervock. He called for the horse and returned home at 7.45pm, feeding the animal before having supper himself. None of the family remembered him bringing the gun he had bought a few hours earlier into the house.

About 8.30pm, the Gardners, with the exception of Jane, were sitting in their kitchen when suddenly Mrs Gardner let out a scream after spotting a face peering in the window at them. She and the old farmer rushed out the front door to see who was there. The servant boy Rodgers, meanwhile, had the sense to go to the window, where he saw Gilmour heading off across the fields. Possibly realising he had been spotted, Gilmour changed direction and instead confronted the Gardners at the front of the house. "Are you going to lay the blame of this wean on me?" he demanded to know. They were not accusing him, the Gardners told Gilmour, but their daughter had named him as the father. Gilmour hit back with an accusation of his own. "I will teach you there are many more fathers than one of that child," he said. He demanded to know if the old man intended taking him to court over the claims, but couldn't get a satisfactory answer. After a further exchange of words, the conversation was broken off and Gilmour apparently headed off. Approximately 20 minutes later the fatal shot was fired through the same window Gilmour had been spotted at earlier.

Within minutes of the shooting, in an apparent bid to establish an alibi, Gilmour was at the door of Samuel Wilson, a labourer who worked for his father. He stayed there for close on two hours before returning home. The police, meanwhile, had been summoned to the Gardners, with Sergeant John Slattery and two constables arriving at the scene shortly before midnight. It didn't take them long to establish who their chief suspect was, and they were soon crossing the short distance to the Gilmour's farm, where they found the young man in bed. A search of his coat quickly turned up the powder and shot bought earlier. His biggest mistake, however, was volunteering the information that he had been at Samuel Wilson's at nine o'clock - for no-one had mentioned when Lyle Gardiner had been shot. Gilmour was promptly arrested and imprisoned in Crumlin Road jail. The murder weapon was found a few days later, hidden in gorse bushes within 300 yards of the Gardners' house.

Gilmour appeared before Mr Justice Gibson at the County Antrim Assizes in July, 1894. As was normal in murder trials, the court was crowded long before the defendant appeared, with people thronging the doorways. Throughout the two-day hearing Gilmour sat forward in the dock, apparently paying great attention to the proceedings, though not displaying any obvious understanding of his predicament. The jury retired at 1.15pm on Thursday, 19th July, returning at 2.45pm with a verdict of guilty, but with a strong recommendation of mercy because of his youth and previous good character. As the judge donned the black cap and delivered his sentence of death, Gilmour alone in the packed courtroom appeared unaffected by the solemnity of the moment.

The day of execution was set for Friday, 18th August, 1894. For the first time in the history of hangings in Belfast, the Press were excluded. The decision by the prison authorities was consistent with a policy being adopted by governors across the British Isles, prompted by the Home Office, and was aimed at putting a stop to newspaper reports of botched executions.

Gilmour, who was guarded by two warders throughout his imprisonment, is said to have slept fairly well on his last night. At 5am, when the Governor visited the condemned cell, he was already up and dressed. An hour later the two Presbyterian clergy who had attended him throughout, the Rev Dr Crawford and the Rev Joseph Northey, arrived at the prison and remained with Gilmour to the end. He breakfasted "very sparingly" on tea and toast and thanked everyone for their care and kindness during his last days. Gilmour is also said to have confessed his guilt. A few minutes before 8am, he shook hands with the Governor, the warders who had made up his guard day and night, and the two clergymen. The usual solemn procession was then formed, with Dr Crawford offering up the prayers from the front and Gilmour, flanked by two warders and walking "with a firm step", joining in. As they approached the scaffold, Scott, the executioner, stepped out from one of the cells and quickly pinioned his arms. The party then passed through a doorway on to the scaffold platform. As the hangman completed his preparations, Gilmour prayed: "Lord, have mercy on my soul; into Thy hands I commend my spirit." As the bolt was drawn, he is said to have called out: "Farewell to all till we meet again."

The scaffold, as for McKeown, had been erected at the end of the prison's D wing, nearest the Mater Hospital, with the condemned cell some 30ft away. The hoisting of the black flag immediately afterwards, and the ringing of the prison bell either side of the execution, let the large crowd gathered outside on the Crumlin Road know that Gilmour had paid the ultimate price for his crime. All but a handful of the people had disappeared by the time the 10am inquest was convened. The jurors, before being sworn in, were taken to the condemned cell to see the body, which had hung for an hour before being taken down and placed in a coffin. They were also shown the gallows and had its workings explained to them by a warder. Back in the boardroom, they were assured by the prison doctor, Dr Stewart, that death had been "almost instantaneous". He refused to be drawn on an exact time but estimated it had taken Gilmour less than three minutes to die. City Coroner E S Finnigan, in an unusual step for a man in his position, went on the record to oppose captial punishment. Pointing out that in previous years hangings had been in public, a "disgrace to their common humanity," he said he felt sure that some, if not all the jurors, probably wished they had been banned altogether rather than merely performed out of sight. The jury, ruling that the death was legal, decided to send letters of sympathy to both the Gilmour and Gardner families.

CHAPTER NINE

New century, old habits

Oh, it is not as bad as a bad marriage.

William Woods
(Condemned man)

THE COUNTY DERRY MURDER.

WOODS PLEADS GUILTY.

SPECIAL TELEGRAM.

DERRY, TUESDAY.—To-day a magisterial investigation into the brutal murder of a woman, which took place a few miles from Londonderry on Sunday last was held. The Court sat in Claudy, and the prisoner, who was arrested yesterday, after hiding without food in a plantation for two days, was put forward, and charged with the wilful murder of Mary Woods, *alias* Irwin. Evidence given that the prisoner and the murdered woman, though both married to other living individuals, had cohabited for nine or ten years. A daughter of the deceased, after severe cross-examination, admitted having heard the prisoner several times threaten to have her mother's life. In reply to a question why she refused to answer at first, the girl said she did not want to be too hard on the murderer. Other evidence as to frequent quarrels between the two was then given. It was also proved that the man and woman were seen approaching the place where the dead body of the latter was afterwards found, and the prisoner's clothes, all blood-stained, were produced. Crooks, the farmer in whose outhouse the woman was found, was being examined, when the prisoner interposed, and said—There is no use keeping you any more. It was I did it. I killed the woman, and that is all there is about it. There need not be any more talk. The prisoner was cautioned, but repeated his statement. Medical evidence was then given, and the inquiry was adjourned till Monday next. The prisoner was removed to Derry Jail.

Woods was fortunate to escape with his life after being convicted of cutting the throat of his common-law wife with a scythe. His luck ran out, however, when he committed a chillingly similar killing a decade later (News Letter).

Execution of William Woods
11th January, 1901

THE MOST remarkable thing about the hanging of William Woods on Friday, 11th January, 1901, was that it had not taken place a decade earlier. With perhaps one other unproven exception, the 58-year-old tramp was the only man executed at Crumlin Road jail who had killed before the murder which finally booked his appointment with the executioner.

Woods' story, for our purposes, begins some 11 years before his death. Described as a dealer, in reality he and common-law wife Mary Irwin were down-and-outs who travelled around County Londonderry gathering rags and reselling them to finance their alcoholism. The pair, both of whom were separated from their respective spouses, had been together for some nine years by 1890. On 5th July that year, a Saturday, they were arrested within an hour of each other for drunkeness in the village of Claudy, and taken to the local barracks to sleep it off. After some six hours in the police cells, they were released together shortly before midnight, and were last seen wandering off towards Londonderry.

As events were to show, they found shelter that night in a shed at Gortnaran, about a mile from Claudy. At 3.15am a farmer, Samuel Crooks, was awakened by what he thought was a scream. He got out of bed and peered from his window into the darkness, but could see nothing unusual and so returned to his slumbers. A few hours later, and with his working day well under way, Crooks went to collect his cart from the shed. There he was confronted by a sight so horrific it would have turned the strongest of stomachs. Mary Irwin, her throat cut, lay in a pool of blood on the floor. Her head, held against the cart wheel by a rope tied in a noose around her neck, stared straight ahead, while the torso lay on one shoulder. A scythe, found on the other side of the cart, was still dripping with her blood.

The next day, in what must have been a harrowing ordeal, Mary's 19-year-old daughter, Matilda Irwin, was brought to the shed from her home in Fountain Street, Londonderry, to identify her mother's body - which had been left as it had been found, still tied to the cart. She also attended an inquest, held in Crooks' farmhouse, where jurors were told the fatal wound had partially separated two vertebrae, finishing perhaps an inch short of decapitation. Meanwhile, 30 RIC officers in plain clothes scarred the countryside for Woods, who had not been seen since leaving Claudy barracks. After spending two days hiding in a haystack, he was eventually captured by Head Constable Webster after hunger forced him out into the open. When arrested he was still wearing the heavily blood-stained clothes he had had on when he cut Mary's throat.

Justice, no matter what else could be said about it, was swift. On 8th July, within hours of being captured, Woods was brought before a magistrate in Claudy to see if he had a case to answer. It was a short sitting. Woods, in what proved to be a typical gesture, brought matters to a speedy conclusion when he interrupted farmer Crooks' evidence to tell the court: "There is no use keeping you any more. It was I did it. I killed the woman, and that is all there is about it. There need not be any more talk." On 22nd July the scene switched to the Crown Court and the Londonderry Assizes. The evidence was damning and it took the jury just 15 minutes to come back with a verdict of guilty - but of manslaughter, not murder. Mr Justice Johnson, in sentencing him to 12 years in jail, told Woods he had that day "stood face-to-face with death," and his escape had been a narrow one. Woods was no stranger to jail, and had more than 30 convictions to his name. He also bragged to officers, while in Claudy barracks the night before the killing, that he had been thrown into police cells some 159 times - not necessarily an accurate figure, but a clear indication of the type of life he led.

With remission, Woods was released from jail in July 1899 and quickly returned to his old ways, but this time his hunting ground was County Antrim. Instead of rags, he now peddled in needles and pins. He often stayed in the Bushmills area and it was there he became friendly with a widow, Bridget McGivern, with whom he often called and occasionally stayed. On the afternoon of 25th September, 1900, Woods bought a razor at Taggart's shop in Bushmills, paying one shilling and sixpence for it. It was, apparently, an investment for he told the assistant who served him that he intended selling it on to a customer in the country. He then headed out to the McGivern cabin at Eagry, on the fringes of the town, where he waited with the widow's children, both boys aged 14 and three, until their mother's arrival about 6.30pm. Woods joined the family for tea and then settled down in front of the fire with a bottle of whiskey, pouring the widow a glass and drinking the rest himself. When that was done, he pulled a further half-pint bottle from inside his coat and, again pouring a tot for Mrs McGivern, consumed the remainder. Woods was evidently in good form, giving the elder boy, Charles, a penny as reward for going for water and later 6d to go to see a menagerie coming to Bushmills. Eventually it was time to retire, the woman sleeping with the two children in one bed and Woods, having taken off his coat and boots, lying on top of the only other bed.

Shortly before 6am the next morning, the oldest boy awoke to discover his mother was no longer lying with him and his brother. Squinting in the cold dawn light, he could just make out a figure lying on the other bed. Realising it was his mother, he went over and tried to rouse her, her flesh warm to the touch. But his mother would never waken again for her throat had been cut. Grabbing the younger child he rushed from the house and across to a neighbour, Matilda Curry, banging on her door and shouting: "For God's

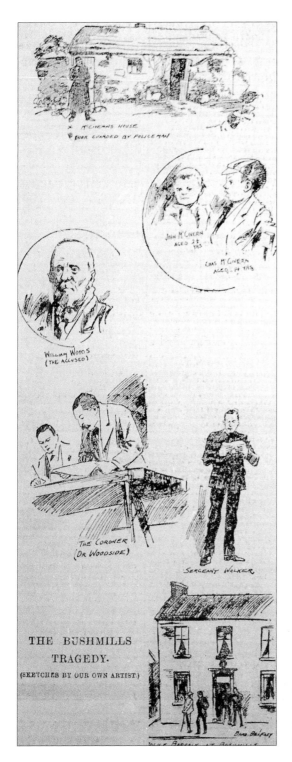

The Belfast Telegraph, then owned by W & G Baird, sent an artist to Bushmills to record the inquest into Bridget McGivern's death.

sake let me and the child in, for Willie Woods has cut the head of me ma." Mrs Curry set out to Bushmills to alert the police, but met a party of officers already on their way. About the same time the boy had found his mother's body, Woods had arrived at the barracks. Smelling of alcohol and covered in blood, he told the sergeant: "The woman in Eagry is dead. I killed the woman, and that is all there is about it. We were both drunk. There is the blood."

The police found Mrs McGivern's body lying partially on its left side, her throat cut "ear to ear". She was almost naked, apart for a strip of a nightdress across her shoulders and covering one breast. Blood was everywhere but concentrated on the chest, face and neck. Oddly, two half-crowns lay in the blood on the bed. Woods' muffler had been thrown across her throat and his coat propped up her head. A postmortem examination showed the throat wound to be $8^1/2$ inches long. As before, it had penetrated right to the vertebral column, just short of completely removing the head. There was also a wound on the left arm about three inches in length.

One can only speculate as to what happened that morning. The fire in the house, raked out the previous evening, had been re-lit, presumably by Mrs McGivern. Perhaps she disturbed Woods while about this task and he attacked her, possibly with rape in mind judging by the state of the woman's night clothes. That, however, would suggest a struggle and there was no evidence of that, not even a scream to waken the children or neighbours. Perhaps the sleeping Woods had been reliving the nightmare of the previous killing, and it had turned into an re-enactment on this poor woman. Or maybe he was simply insane at the time, as his defence was to argue later in court, and didn't know what he was doing. Interestingly, he washed his hands in a bucket of cold water after the killing. He also disposed of the razor in a derelict building (it was found on 17th November, 1900, by some children and handed over to the RIC) close to the police station before giving himself up. Again it can only be guess work, but Woods may have been thinking of making a run for it until he realised how desperate was his plight.

On 12th December, 1900, William Woods stood trial in front of Mr Justice Madden at the Ulster Winter Assizes. The jury took half-an-hour to find him guilty of murder and his execution date was set for 11th January, 1901. As he left the dock, Woods uttered the immortal line: "Oh, it is not as bad as a bad marriage." This apparent indifference continued throughout his three weeks in the condemned cell, with Woods joking with his warders as to the quality of whiskey he would receive in jail. He also ate heartily, putting on 20lbs between his conviction and death. As the day of execution grew closer, however, and any hopes of a reprieve faded, Woods grew depressed, refusing to eat altogether in his last few days. He also began taking a greater interest in the spiritual offerings of the Church of Ireland chaplain, the Rev Dr Spence, who as custom demanded spent the last few hours with the condemned man.

At 8am, executioner Scott entered the cell and pinioned Woods' arms. He was led, with the help of two warders, the few yards onto the gallows. With no assistant, the hangman completed the process on his own, securing the legs, placing the white hood over the head and adjusting the rope about the neck. As Scott stood back to push the lever,

Woods muttered a few lines of prayer before he was launched into eternity. At 5ft 5½ ins and weighing 133lbs on the day of execution, he was given a drop of some 7ft 10ins. The tolling of the prison bell and the hoisting of the black flag told the crowd outside the prison walls, made up mainly of the "lower classes," that the execution had been carried out. After hanging for the usual hour, the body was taken down and placed in a black painted coffin, lined with wood shavings. Woods was dressed in a rough brown jacket, dark trousers and black socks. Shortly after 11am, the corpse was inspected by the inquest jury. Journalists were also admitted at this point and one recorded:

> *The deceased was fully dressed in his own clothes, excepting his boots, hat and collar, and it was quite evident that when the neck was dislocated a quantity of blood issued from his nose. His face was slightly bulged, and his left eye partially open. It was difficult to see the mark of the rope on the neck in consequence of his beard - indeed, there was little to make one believe that he had not died a natural death.*

Dr John Stewart, the prison doctor, agreed it had been a textbook hanging: "It appeared to be most skilful. I am prepared to say death was instantaneous. There was not a quiver of a muscle of the body."

ALEXANDRA PARK, BELFAST. 3866. W.L.

Alexandra Park was opened in 1887 on a 10-acre site. A further 10 acres were purchased in 1908 and a team of workmen, including Richard Justin, laboured to reshape it as part of a relief works scheme. It was from Alexandra Park that Justin returned to his New Lodge home the morning little Annie was found barely alive (Laurence collection, National Library of Ireland).

Execution of Richard Justin
19th August, 1909

BRIDGET McWILLIAMS was the salt of the earth. While most other people were prepared to turn their backs on an unmarried mother, she went out of her way to help. Every morning for four years she took on the role of unpaid nanny to Annie Thompson, taking the girl into her own home to allow her mother, Jane, to continue working. Even after the belated marriage of the child's parents, Mrs McWilliams continued to look after little Annie on a daily basis. She began to become alarmed, however, after noticing bruising on the four-year-old's body. There were other injuries, too, including a swollen chin, a black eye and a tooth apparently knocked out. But, in February, 1909, just as her concern began to grow into a genuine fear for the child's safety, Annie was stopped coming to Mrs McWilliams house, staying home instead.

That home was in Lepper Street, in the New Lodge area of Belfast. She shared it with her father, Richard Justin, her mother, and two half-brothers. The first Mrs Justin had died some eight years earlier, before the relationship began which produced Annie out of wedlock.

On 12th March, 1909, Jane Justin left the house at 6am as normal to go to work in Whitehouse Mill, to be followed five minutes later by her husband. He, like so many others, was finding it difficult to get a regular job but had been given a place working on the Belfast Corporation relief works for the unemployed in Alexandra Park. Justin returned home at 9am, apparently for breakfast. But within minutes of his arrival he was at the door of Annie Loughlands, who lived in an upstairs room of the same house. His daughter, he told her, had fallen out of bed and was in urgent need of help. While the neighbour stayed with Annie, Justin went off in search of a doctor. It was to no avail. The child, who was unconscious throughout, died at 10.50am. She was three months short of her fifth birthday.

Within hours of the death the rumours began to fly around. Some told of screaming and crying coming from the house; others of the marks seen on the child's body; and all pointed the finger at the father. A postmortem, carried out the next day, seemed to confirm the stories, for the doctors found a litany of injuries. These included some 30 bruises to the chest, arms, thighs and head, though most were several days old. Prof Symmers, who conducted the medical investigation, even went as far as to say they were the worst injuries to a child he had ever seen. Following his evidence at the inquest on 15th March, Justin was arrested and charged with murder.

The case came to trial at the City of Belfast Assizes on 22nd July, 1909. The prosecution, alleging that Annie's death was the cumulation of months of abuse with the intention of causing her to die, produced a series of witnesses to back the assertion. One neighbour told the court she had heard Annie's mother, Jane Justin, cry out on one occasion: "Hit me, and let the child alone," while another, Margaret Craig, who claimed Justin had regularly beat the girl when left alone with her, said she had heard Annie cry out: "Da, da, don't beat me anymore." A work colleague of Mrs Justin's, Annie McGeough, was called to repeat Jane's reaction to being told by Justin that Annie had been hurt: "I knew you would finish her at last." Several "weapons" found in the Justin household, including a piece of wood and an iron rod, were also produced, with allegations made that they were used to beat the child, though there was no evidence to support the claim.

The defence rested on the testimony of Justin's eldest son, also called Richard. He said the three children – himself, his younger brother Jack and Annie – had been lying in the one bed, with the little girl nearest the wall. Shortly before 7am, Annie had awakened and began climbing over the boys to get out of bed. She had trampled on the edge of her nightdress, however, and fell over the side. Her head, he said in evidence, had struck the metal strut of their parents' bed, which was only separated from the children's bed by about 18 inches. The girl had let out a moan and then lay still on the floor. Richard, picking her up, gently set her back in the bed, being careful not to waken his brother. It was there that his father had found her some two hours later, he told a hushed court. Richard also denied his father beat the girl, but instead accused his stepmother's sister, also named Annie Thompson, of banging the girl's head against a wall several days before the youngster's death. Prof Symmers, who again presented his evidence, admitted a fall as described by Richard could have resulted in the brain haemorrhage which caused death. Asked to speculate, however, he came up with the theory that a blow struck with the iron bar found in the house had caused the fatal injury.

In conclusion, the jurors were asked to avoid the "natural prejudice" felt towards a man accused of killing a child. They retired at 7.45pm and returned 45 minutes later with a guilty verdict. The defence, with some justification, considered Justin hadn't been given the benefit of what appeared to be a reasonable doubt. There was a possibility, it was felt, that the jury had believed him guilty of scheming to kill the child, and that the plot had not succeeded only because of an unfortunate accident. In other words, even if he hadn't actually murdered Annie, there was no reason to consider him innocent when he had an evil intent towards the girl. A petition sent to the Lord Lieutenant asking for a reprieve was turned down, and Justin was left to face his last days in the condemned cell at Crumlin Road.

Little is known of the execution itself, carried out on 19th August, 1909, apparently without any unusual incidents. The Rev Frederick Woolley, of the Unitarian Mission on Belfast's Stanhope Street, shared Justin's last few hours, reading him prayers and offering solace up until the release of the gallows trap doors a few seconds after eight o'clock. A fair size crowd had gathered outside the prison, filling the Crumlin Road between the jail and courthouse. There was even less for them to see than at previous executions, however,

LFAST MORNING NEWS, FRIDAY, AUGUST 20, 1

THE EXTREME PENALTY.

Richard Justin Executed in Belfast Jail.

PRISONER'S PENITENCE.

CONDEMNED MAN THANKS COUNSEL FOR ABLE DEFENCE.

The wretched man, Richard Justin, who was condemned to death for the wilful murder of his child at the recent Summer Assizes, suffered the extreme penalty of the law at the Belfast Jail yesterday morning. Since his condemnation Justin exhibited great penitence, and was most attentive to the ministrations of his clergyman, the Rev. Mr. Woolley, Unitarian minister. Shortly before eight o'clock Mr. Thomas Stringer, Governor of the Prison, formally handed Justin over to the custody of the High Sheriff (Councillor F. Curley, J.P.) and the Sub-Sheriff (Mr. James Quail). Pierpont, the executioner, then took charge of the prisoner, and commenced his gruesome task. It was but a short distance from the cell to the execution room. Justin, it is said, displayed remarkable fortitude; and so expeditiously did the executioner carry out his

DREADFUL PRELIMINARIES

that in an almost incredibly short space of time the bolt was drawn, and the wretched man launched into eternity. After hanging for some time the body was cut down, and placed in a rough deal shell, in which it was subsequently viewed by the jury previous to the inquest. Outside the jail people, prompted by morbid curiosity, commenced to assemble from an early hour, and from seven o'clock onward the crowd was every moment augmented, many being evidently under the impression that they would witness the hoisting of the sinister black flag. As this custom was abolished some years ago the first intimation to the waiting crowd that

THE GRIM LEGAL TRAGEDY

was complete was the tolling of the prison bell. A little time afterwards the notices required by law were posted on the main gate of the prison buildings. Of these notices there were three. The first announced that the execution would take place at the hour specified, and was posted the previous night. Another, signed by the High Sheriff, Sub-Sheriff, the Governor of the jail, and the clergyman in attendance on the condemned man, declared that the "judgment of death" had been carried out. The third and final notice was a certificate from Dr. Stewart, medical officer of the prison, announcing that "the said Richard Justin was dead."

So far as can be ascertained, Justin met his death with great penitence and fortitude. His farewell to his aged and sorrow-stricken father and mother was piteously painful, and the prison officials whose duty compelled them to be present at the final leave-taking between the condemned man and his relatives were much affected by the scenes of grim and sorrowing grief. One of the

LAST ACTS OF THE CONDEMNED MAN

was to send to his surviving children a number of books which had been presented to him by friends since his sentence. He expressed unbounded gratitude to Mr. Thomas J. Campbell, B.L., who ably and eloquently defended him at his trial, and desired that a sincere message of thanks should be conveyed to that gentleman. Justin atoned for a shocking crime with his life, and in the days that were left him since his condemnation, he undoubtedly expressed deep penitence for the offence that rendered forfeit his existence, and showed his gratitude for the acts of kindness and consideration extended him by the prison officials.

The Inquest.

Dr. James Graham, City Coroner, opened an inquest on the remains in the Boardroom of the Prison yesterday, and a jury, of which Alderman W. Tougher, J.P., was foreman, viewed the body.

walls of the said prison, on the 19th day of August, 1909, not more than twenty-tours before the holding of this inquest, and that the body on which this inquest was held is the identical body of the said Richard Justin, adjudged to death as aforesaid."

Subsequent to the inquest the remains were interred within the precincts of the jail.

Justin's Crime—Counsel's Eloquent Appeal.

The history of the crime for which Justin paid the extreme penalty is too fresh in the minds of our readers to need recapitulation. In view of his penitence and his expressions of deep gratitude to Mr. Campbell, B.L., for his able defence, it may not be out of place to give the following extracts from counsel's able and eloquent appeal to the jury:—

The Crown, said Mr. Campbell, asked them to say that the prisoner's hands were crimson with the blood of his infant daughter—a crime most foul, cruel, and unnatural, which would cry aloud from earth to Heaven for vengeance. Let them pause and think long and well of what the learned Attorney-General asked them to do—to find him guilty of the destruction, the deliberate destruction of his own child—blood of his blood, bone of his bone—and for no reason. Theirs was the awful duty of sitting in judgment upon life and death. The slow, sure passage of the clock that summer day might have reminded some among them that we are all passing on to the last Assize of all—to the Judgment Throne of the great King of Kings, in Whose sight a thousand years are as yesterday which is past and as a watch in the night. In the eternal tables of His law the Divine Judge has decreed that human life was sacred beyond all gold and silver and precious stones. Little Annie Thompson had passed before that Judgment Throne, and death would be no more for her, nor mourning nor sorrow any more. Could they in their consciences

VISIT HER DEATH ON HER OWN FATHER?

The law for the protection of the good and the repression of the wicked would adjudge that a crime of that crimson dye, upon one so young, so helpless, so tender, deserved the last dread penalty—that blood should atone for blood, and life should pay for life. Their verdict of "Guilty" would mean for the prisoner that, after three or four weeks of agony in the gloom of his condemned cell, a death of shame would await him, and his eyes would never again open to the sun and sky. He (counsel) spoke, therefore, as one who felt he was standing between this man and the scaffold. With all earnestness he begged and implored them to raise their minds high and clear above prejudice. He feared the prejudice which sprung up irresistibly in favour of a weak child alleged to have been

DONE TO DEATH BY A STRONG MAN.

Let the jury pay no regard to anything but the voice of their own consciences and sense of their duty to God and man. In the dreadful straits in which the prisoner now stood he was not deserted by his family. His father, broken with years—who, he (counsel) prayed, would not be broken hereafter with shame—had told them on his oath that the prisoner was a maligned man, and far from being a cruel man, was kind to the dead child. They had heard that bright little fellow, Richard, to whom the man in the dock was never a cruel father. Prisoner's wife was in that court, and of all living beings she could speak best on this awful charge, but the law sealed her mouth. She must sit in silence. She could not go into the witness-box to tell the jury what she knew of it all. What a hard fate was hers! Upon the evidence before them the jury could not, they ought not to, they dared not find the prisoner guilty. They would vindicate their character and honour as

FEARLESS GUARDIANS OF JUSTICE

—justice perpetual and immortal. The Crown asked for that verdict of guilty that would, within a month, by the hand of man, take from the prisoner the life which had been lent him, and which God would ask for again in His own good time, when this man's dust would return to the earth from whence it came, and his soul return to the Maker Who gave it—He (counsel) asked unhesitatingly and unfalteringly for a verdict of not guilty, and with reverence and with humble heart he prayed that the spirit of justice would be amongst them,

How the Irish News reported Justin's execution

for the custom of hoisting a black flag immediately the condemned man was pronounced dead had been abandoned in the intervening years since Woods' execution. The prison bell was still rung and was still tolling when a warder appeared at the doors to nail up a notice, signed by High Sheriff Francis Curley, Under Sheriff James Quail, Thomas Stringer the Governor and Mr Woolley, stating the "judgment of death" had been carried out. A certificate of death, signed by Dr John Stewart, the prison doctor, was also posted. An inquest, opened by city coroner Dr James Graham at 10am in the Governor's room at the jail, heard that Justin had walked firmly to the scaffold and had shown great remorse for his crime. Death, Dr Stewart assured the jurors, had been instantaneous. A few hours later Justin's body joined the others alongside the graveyard wall.

CHAPTER TEN

TROUBLED TIMES

God was good to you, for if you had been near the premises you would have been shot too.

William Smiley
(Murderer)

CAVEHILL, BELFAST. 1992. W.L.

The grounds of Belfast Castle, seen in the
distance just right of centre in this photograph
taken from the Cavehill Road, was where the
body of seven-year-old Maggie Fullerton was
discovered (Laurence collection,
National Library of Ireland).

Execution of Simon McGeown
17th August, 1922

FOR DAYS Robert Fullerton walked the streets of north Belfast in the vain hope he would find his seven-year-old daughter. With every passing hour, and the fruitless searches of entries and empty houses, his distress had grown more acute. Maggie was a good girl and he knew she wouldn't just wander off like that. In his heart the father knew he would never see his little girl alive again. Fullerton called on neighbours, asking if they had seen the child. He talked to her friends and he regularly checked with the police in case they had news. But for four days there was nothing. Then came the knock at his door he had feared the most. Maggie was dead, the victim of a sex pervert.

It was on the Tuesday evening of 30th May, 1922, about 6pm, that Fullerton last saw her alive at the family's Little Henry Street home. He had given her twopence to buy sweets from the corner shop. An hour later, when he went out to bring her in for the night, she was nowhere to be seen. It wasn't until the Saturday that the distressed father was to set eyes on his daughter again, when he identified her battered and bloodied corpse as it lay on a morgue dissecting table.

The body had been found by Samuel Armstrong, a gamekeeper working for Lord Shaftesbury on his Cave Hill demense. He had been in the estate's pine plantation that morning, accompanied by his faithful hound, hoping to kill a hawk which was preying on small birds in the area. However, when he called the dog to his side it refused to come. Puzzled by the animal's unusual behaviour, he went to investigate, and immediately spotted the cause of the dog's reluctance. Beneath a pile of rubbish and leaves lay a child's body, with the feet clearly visible. Within an hour the plantation was swarming with policemen and the hunt for the killer underway.

A few days later, on 7th June, Belfast City Coroner Dr J Graham held an inquest into the death. It was a harrowing tale. The doctor who had carried out the postmortem gave details of his findings. The little seven-year-old, he told a hushed court, had been brutally raped and then savagely battered and stabbed. A gaping wound measuring two inches by an inch was in her abdomen and her skull was fractured in several places, either as a result of being repeatedly kicked or being struck with a blunt instrument. It was these latter injuries which had caused death. In addition, her body was covered in a mass of bruises and fingernail scratches. The abandoned corpse had also attracted the attentions of the estate's wildlife, with the left foot badly gnawed by rats and the eyes and part of the forehead eaten away by field maggots. The inquest recorded a verdict of "murder by some unknown person," but it was a mystery the police were already well on their way to solving. Within 24 hours of the inquest closing, a 38-year-old man named Simon McGeown, who was already being held in police custody on another charge, was positively identified by three witnesses as having been with Maggie on the day of her disappearance.

Born near Lurgan, McGeown had joined the army as a young man and was soon drafted to India, where he served with distinction until struck down in quick succession by sunstroke, malaria and intestine problems. There after his military career went rapidly downhill and he regularly found himself before his superiors on a variety of petty charges. Once out of the army again, he returned to Ireland where he had difficulty settling back into civilian life. The start of the First World War, in August 1914, gave him the opportunity to re-enlist, which he did within a week. With his previous training to his credit, McGeown was rapidly processed and on a boat to France to help stabilise the British lines. Wounded at least twice, and suffering the effects of gas attacks, he was discharged from the army as unfit to serve and again found himself back in Ireland without a job or prospects. Over the next few years he was to be arrested and charged on half-a-dozen occasions for a range of offences, including breaking and entering, larceny and receiving stolen goods. In total, he had spent some 30 months in jail up until being charged with Maggie's murder.

On 22 July, some six weeks after being charged, McGeown took his place in the dock of the Belfast City Commission before Lord Justice Andrews. His trial was to take just the one day. The former soldier stood rigidly to attention when asked to plead. Described in the newspapers as a "strong muscular-looking man," he attempted to put in as respectable an appearance as possible. His black hair was well brushed, and he was dressed in a grey suit and shirt, though without a collar or tie.

The court heard how McGeown, who had been staying in a lodging house in Henry Street at the time of the murder, was constantly in trouble with the law. An alcoholic, he had spent most of 30th May, the day of Maggie's disappearance, drinking methylated spirits. His thirst, no doubt, had increased on hearing police officers had called at his lodgings asking about him. McGeown decided to move on.

A 13-year-old girl, Annie Addis, of Ellen's Court, told how McGeown had approached her and a friend about 6.30pm that evening and asked her to go with him to collect clothes from a woman on the Limestone Road. McGeown had told her the woman wouldn't part with the items unless he was accompanied by "his little girl". Annie insisted she ask her mother first, and ran home. Ten minutes later, when she came back, she saw McGeown with Maggie Fullerton in Henry Street. The girl was holding his hand as they walked to his lodging house to collect his belongings. The two then strolled along Henry Street towards York Street. A second girl, Maggie Larkham, who lived close to the murdered child in Little Henry Street, also saw the pair walking towards York Street. She called out: "Come on back out of that, Maggie," but the girl just looked round and laughed.

The Belfast Castle estate, with its views over the
city and beyond, was where Simon McGeown
brutally raped then beat to death his child victim
(Laruence collection, National Library of Ireland).

Simon McGeown, a former soldier who had
served during the First World War, was convicted
of the murder of a little girl and sentenced to be
hanged at Crumlin Road Jail.

133

At 7pm, the all-male jury (women had been asked to "stand by" because of the distressing nature of the evidence) retired to make their judgment. Less than an hour later they returned with a guilty verdict. Asked if he had anything to say before the sentence of death was passed, McGeown could only manage to whisper: "I have nothing to say, sir." The judge donned the black cap and set the execution date for 17th August. McGeown was the first man to face the gallows in the newly-formed State of Northern Ireland and as such the issue of whether or not a reprieve was in order came before the Cabinet at a meeting in Stormont Castle on Wednesday, 9th August, 1922. Among those present were the Prime Minister, Sir James Craig, Minister of Home Affairs, Sir Richard Dawson, the Minister of Labour, J M Andrews and the Minister of Education, the Marquess of Londonderry. The Inspector General of the Royal Ulster Constabulary, Charles Wickham, was also in attendance. The minutes of that meeting, although adding little in terms of information, are worth including as the file is the only one at which a death sentence was discussed currently open. All others are closed for 100 years from the date of the relevant meetings. It read:

> The Cabinet decided to communicate to the Lord Lieutenant the circumstances of the case of Simon McGeown although no petition against sentence had been forwarded. The recommendation of the Cabinet was that there were no circumstances in the case which warranted mitigation of the sentence.

By 7.30am on 17th August, the bulk of more than 2,000 people who were to gather outside the jail had already taken up position. Mostly they were women and children, though a large contingent were men who had stopped off on their way to work. There was little for them to see until a warder appeared shortly after 8am to post a notice declaring the execution had taken place. At that point the police, who had held the crowd away from the prison doors, stood back to allow the sign to be read. In the crush to get into the narrow passageway, a number of people were slightly injured and the shrieks of terrified women and girls could be heard across the Crumlin Road.

Inside the prison, McGeown had reportedly went to his death with apparently the "unflinching demeanour which he had manifested at his trial," much to the relief of his executioner, Ellis, who was assisted by Willis. McGeown had freely admitted his guilt to warders, though in the same breath claimed to remember nothing of what he was alleged to have done. At 10 o'clock, an inquest was held within the jail and shortly afterwards the body of Simon McGeown was lowered into an unmarked grave.

Execution of Michael Pratley
8th May, 1924

NELSON LEECH was a man who took his responsibilities very seriously, even to the point of being prepared to lay down his life rather than give up his employer's money. A book-keeper at Messrs Purdy and Millard's sculptor works on College Square North, Belfast, it was his job to collect the cash from the bank every Friday so the wage packets, handed out on Saturday morning, could be prepared. It was an important task that only an experienced and trusted man would be allowed to do, and so it was with a sense of pride that Mr Leech ran his weekly errand. On 7th March, 1924, he set off as usual to the Ulster Bank offices in nearby Queen Street, returning a short time later with a bag of notes and small change. But that particular Friday was far from usual. No sooner was he back in his office when the doors burst open and three men, wearing masks and carrying guns, ran in, ordering the staff to put their hands up. Mr Leech, however, was not prepared to be intimidated and in turn ordered the men out of the office. He then turned and ran towards a telephone box in the room to summon help. The raiders were now in a dilemma. What had started out as a straight-forward wages snatch was turning into a farce. What was worse, there was now the distinct possibility that the alarm was going to be raised before they even had a chance to lay a finger on the cash. They had to think quickly and on their feet. Either they turned and ran empty-handed, or they took action. Unfortunately they choose the latter. One of the raiders fired a warning shot over Mr Leech's head, but he continued into the phone box and picked up the receiver. A second man tried to pull him out and a scuffle developed. Mr Leech grabbed for the gun but missed – and suffered the consequences. From a range of less than six inches the gunman fired. The farce had become a tragedy, and all three raiders took to their heels.

While Alexander Briggs, a company clerk, ran to the shot man's aid, another employee, Miss Elizabeth Allen, gave chase. The trio had split up, two running down Galway Street and another along Hamill Street. It looked like they were going to make good their getaway, but Miss Allen had other ideas. Reaching College Square barracks she called out to Constable Francis Morteshed, who took up the chase helped by a passer-by who pointed him in the right direction. As the policeman reached Durham Street, he spotted two men heading into Barrack Street, one lagging behind the other. Halfway along, Constable Morteshed caught hold of the slower man, dragging him to a stop. But far from giving up, he whipped round and shoved the barrel of a revolver into the policeman's chest

Photographs from the Belfast Telegraph showing the front of Purdy and Millard's premises, the police officer who arrested Pratley, the inside of the office where the murder took place, College Square police station, and finally Pratley himself and the spot where he was arrested in Barrack Street and pulled the trigger - but the gun failed to fire and he was ultimately disarmed and detained.

The arrested man was 30-year-old Michael Pratley, from Moira Street in the city. A former soldier, he had lost a leg during the Great War and no doubt it was this handicap which impeded his escape. His weapon was found to have been one of those used in the raid, while a search of his house revealed a second revolver. Pratley admitted his part in the attempted robbery, enough in itself to convict him of murder regardless of who fired the fatal shot. Nonetheless, when his case came to trial at the City of Belfast Commission on Thursday, 10th April, 1924, he insisted he had only discharged the warning shot over Mr Leech's head. No doubt he was hoping that if he could convince the court he hadn't actually done the killing, a reprieve might be forthcoming. His case, however, wasn't helped by the admission in evidence of a letter he had written to his wife, Josephine, from his prison cell. It read:

> My Dearest Joe,
>
> I want to say a few things which are best said now. When I stand on my trial it is not unlikely that I may be sentenced to death, and it is best to know it now, instead of coming as a shock later on. This letter is being slipped out, and it would be better to burn it in case it comes into the hands of the police. No matter how the case goes, I hope the two men who were with me will do their best for you. When the trial comes I am going to say that after the shooting I changed guns with one of the others, as his gun was too big to go in his pocket. That was how I had that particular gun.

Faced with overwhelming evidence, and the prisoner's own admission, the jury took less than 30 minutes to return a guilty verdict. Pratley paled slightly but otherwise showed little emotion. Asked if he had anything to say as to why sentence of death should not be passed, he curtly replied: "I have no more to say than I have already said."

On the face of it, Pratley was that rarity of the scaffold; a professional criminal who committed murder. There is another, much more intriguing aspect to the man, however, for two days after he was sentenced to death he had been due to appear back in the same court charged with a second murder - that of Northern Ireland MP William Twaddell, shot dead two years previously.

At about 10.30am on 22nd May, 1922, William Twaddell was making his way from Royal Avenue through Lower Garfield Street towards North Street. As he passed an entry, a group of men stepped out onto the pavement behind him, with one firing a single round into his back. Mr Twaddell fell to his knees, then onto his face. A second member of the group stepped forward and emptied his weapon into the prostrate figure. The gang then scattered, but with both gunmen making their way along Royal Avenue towards Smithfield, firing at least one more round at a man who tried to trip one of them up. A Captain W D Ryall, who had been a police officer in India, heard the shooting as he walked along Castle Junction. Abandoning his attache case in a doorway, he drew out his own weapon and, spotting the gunmen coming into Royal Avenue, fired two shots in their direction before his automatic pistol jammed. At this point a Constable H H Davidson emerged from the Post Office and, seeing Capt Ryall firing at the men, he also began stalking them - though he could have had no idea just why this gun battle was in progress. His gun also jammed, however, and he was forced to give up the pursuit. One of the gunmen, claimed to be Pratley, was said to have had a limp.

In the event, Pratley was not to stand trial for Mr Twaddell's murder, with the Crown entering a *Nolle Prosequi* as a result of the guilty verdict handed down two days previously. His co-accused was James Woods, from Ballyhornan, Ardglass, an officer in the Free State army who had been interned on suspicion of terrorist involvement. He had spent spells in camps in Larne and Londonderry, but it was while in Crumlin Road Jail that he had been picked out of an identity parade by Capt Ryall as the killer of William Twaddell. The case aroused great excitment and a huge crowd turned up at the court. Only the jurors, witnesses and a very select audience were admitted, however, including Major-General O'Connell, chief of staff of the Free State army, who wore civilian clothes to Belfast. The case, of course, rested entirely on the identification evidence against Woods (which seemed weaker than that which Pratley would have faced). Unconvinced, the jury returned a not guilty verdict, though Woods didn't walk free but back into an internment camp.

Unlike Woods, Pratley's time in prison was strictly limited. His execution had been set for Thursday, 8th May and from the outset there had been little hope of a reprieve. The Northern Ireland Cabinet had discussed the possibility on 15th April but decided instead to confirm the sentence two weeks later. A large crowd gathered outside the prison on the appointed day and stood in near silence. A few minutes after 8am, a notice was posted on the prison door informing the onlookers that the death penalty had been duly carried out. Inside, Pratley apparently met his fate with the "stoical demeanour" with which he had approached his entire predicament. He was attended to by Roman Catholic chaplains, who did their best to comfort him in his final hours, though even they could not persuade him to take a last meal or drink. Willis was the executioner and death, according to the prison doctor, was instantaneous.

Pratley took many secrets with him to his grave inside the prison walls, including the names of his fellow gang members and details of any part he may have played in the Twaddell murder. Was he indeed simply a professional criminal who got caught up, almost by accident, in an unplanned murder, or a politically motivated cold-blooded killer? We may never know the full truth.

ANOTHER BELFAST SENSATION

Member of Parliament Murdered.

SHOT DOWN IN CENTRE OF CITY.

Five More Deaths Yesterday.

The great sensation of yesterday was the murder of Councillor W. J. Twaddell, a member of the Northern Parliament, who was shot down in Garfield Street, Belfast, in close proximity to Royal Avenue, the principal thoroughfare of the city.

The crime was perpetrated about half-past ten in the morning. Two or three men were concerned in the attack, and they made their escape, notwithstanding the fact that within a narrow radius there were hundreds of people astir.

A renewal of sniping occurred in the East End, and during the day three men were mortally wounded in that area. At the Midland Railway terminus a ganger was murdered, whilst a rag-picker was killed in Duncrue Street.

An electric clock mine was found in a cable man-hole in Arthur Square. It was timed to explode at two o'clock in the afternoon, and had it not been for a timely discovery very extensive damage would have been done.

GARFIELD STREET CRIME.

Shocking Daylight Tragedy

ASSASSINS' AUDACITY.

Of the many appalling crimes which have shocked the people of Belfast during recent months, none sent a greater thrill of horror through the community than the murder of Councillor W. J. Twaddell, member of Parliament for the West division of Belfast in the Northern Parliament, which took place yesterday morning. Mr. Twaddell was proceeding to his place of business in North Street about half-past-ten o'clock when he was attacked by a number of men in Lower Garfield Street and seven or eight shots fired at him. He fell to the ground mortally wounded and the assassins dashed along Garfield Street and across Royal Avenue on the

EAST END SNIPING.

Three Men Shot Dead.

YORK ROAD MURDERS.

The Ballymacarrett gunmen were active about eleven o'clock yesterday morning, and shots were fired in Altcar Street and Lisbon Street. Some of the snipers came to the corner of the latter thoroughfare and fired in the direction of Albertbridge Road, a man named Thos. Boyd (25) 268 Donegall Road, being shot dead, James Lindsay (18), 4, Cumberland Street, being wounded. Both men were in a cycle agent's shop immediately opposite Lisbon Street, and Boyd, who carries on a licensed business, was hit in the head and fell dead in the doorway. Lindsay, who is a mechanic employed on the

MORE TROO

CHURCHIL

Full Suppo
Gov

THE MURDER

Mr. Churchill had House of Commons, garding Sinn Fein's and the assassinatio M.P.

He said four additiona had been landed i forcements would b the military authori

Captain Craig ask Colonies whether he h the House with refer in Ulster, and particu reported assassination Northern Parliament.

Mr. Churchill, ha (which is reported in ing the new Collins-D on—With regard to Ireland, I regret profo that

I have just recei Prime Minister of that Mr. W. J. Tw Northern Parliamen just been brutally business premises in Apart from this shock add anything to the f peared in the newspap have been organised various parts of the condition of disorder Belfast. I have every ern Government will the serious task of res ditional battalions lan on Saturday, raising t Six Counties to 19 bat

Further reinforcer sent to any extent necessary in the op authorities. (Cheers I am in consultation w Northern Government Londonderry—has bee to discuss with the Go the question of further ment to the police for Government are organ deavour will be made t

The headlines from the Belfast News Letter which told of the daylight shooting of Stormont MP William Twaddell, of which Pratley was later accused.

139

Kate Murdoch, a labourer on the Macauley farm, made the horrific discovery of her mistresses bodies in the kitchen of their Armoy house.

Execution of William Smiley
8th August, 1928

IT WAS early afternoon when Kate Murdoch eventually finished budding the potatoes in the plot close to the farmhouse. It was back-breaking work and she was glad of the opportunity to call back to the house. But the sight which greeted her sent Kate reeling, for on the floor lay the bodies of two women, their blood splattered all over the walls, floor and furniture of the room. Another farm hand, William Smiley, was working the horses in a field nearby and Kate ran to him for help. Re-emerging from the house, he told her: "God was good to you, for if you had been near the premises you would have been shot too." Smiley should have known, for it was he who less than an hour earlier had committed one of the most callous double murders in the history of Belfast executions.

Both Smiley and Kate, along with another labourer, Thomas McCaughan, worked for the Macauley family on their farm about two miles outside Armoy. On the day of the murders, 24th May, 1928, the Macauley brothers, Andrew and Leslie, were repairing a fence some three-quarters of a mile away from the farmhouse, which was known as Mullaghduff Big. Both sisters were at home and it was the younger of the pair, 43-year-old Sarah, who left about 11.30am to bring the men their lunch. Some 20 minutes later, Margaret Macauley called the rest of the workforce into the kitchen for their dinner. Sitting at the head of the table, Margaret kept everyone enthralled by reading extracts from the newspaper of an appeal court hearing by two men, Frederick Browne and William Kennedy, who had earlier been found guilty of the murder of Constable Gutteridge in Essex the previous September. It is hardly likely, though, that the men's predicament spurred Smiley on to hatch his own ill-conceived plan, for they too ended upon the gallows.

Both men left the house at 12.20pm, with McCaughan heading home shortly afterwards. Smiley, who initially went to the stables to prepare the horses to continue the ploughing, then went back to the house. On the kitchen wall was a shotgun which he lifted down, loaded, and turned on 48-year-old Margaret, blasting her in the head. Smiley then raided the bedrooms, taking £30 cash, a gold watch and chain, and some silver. Meanwhile, Sarah was on her way back to the house and had met Kate on the road. The two women walked down together chatting, before separating at the door shortly before 1pm. Once inside, Sarah is believed to have ran to where her sister's body lay, and was leaning over her when Smiley shot her from close range, virtually blasting her head off her

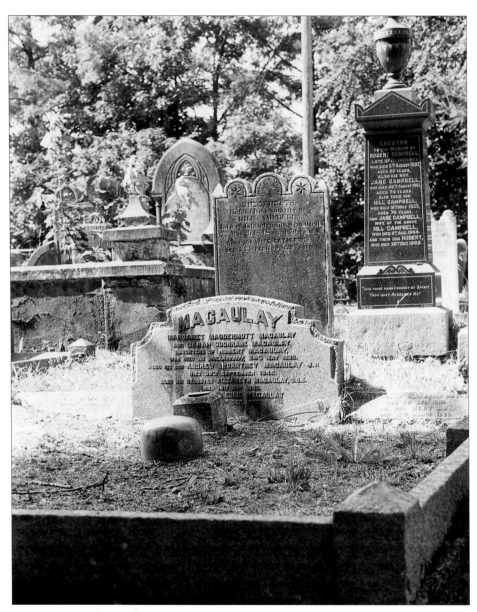

The Macauley family grave lies in the
shade of a tree-lined pathway at
Armoy Presbyterian Church.

shoulders. Kate, heading back to the potato field, heard the shot but thought nothing of it until she discovered the bodies a short time later.

Smiley, keeping up the pretence, walked to Armoy to notify the police about the murders, before retiring to Devlin's pub for a glass of whiskey, which he paid for with one of the halfcrowns he had just stolen. Fortified by the drink, he returned to the farm and crossed the fields to tell the brothers that their sisters had just been murdered: "You are sitting there, and the two girls shot and the gun lying across them and the house raided," he told them.

It is unlikely the police would have looked much further than Smiley, a former soldier with the Royal Irish Rifles, as a suspect even in the normal course of events. His loose tongue, however, soon brought about his downfall. Within earshot of a policeman guarding the entrance of the house, in which the bodies still lay, 28-year-old Smiley and his wife had an argument. "The whole countryside say you did this thing," she challenged him. "I had nothing to do with the murder, I only took the money," he replied. "I might as well have something as the rest of them. They can do nothing but swing me, anyway." Smiley was arrested the next day, and the money found hidden in the sole of his boot. He readily admitted the theft, though maintained he wasn't the killer.

The case came to trial on 10th July, 1928, in front of a packed court. Approximately another 100 people were unable to get inside and milled about in the corridors. Standing impassively in the dock, and dressed in a blue serge suit and a white silk scarf instead of a collar and tie, the slightly-built Smiley appeared to take little interest in the 11 hours of evidence presented. In the witness box himself, he claimed he had helped Margaret - he was only charged with her murder for legal reasons - with a few chores before leaving for the fields. The last time he had seen her she was sitting by the kitchen window reading, he said. The jury retired at 8.45pm and returned just 20 minutes later with a guilty verdict. The Lord Chief Justice, before pronouncing sentence, told Smiley:

> *You gave these unfortunate women no chance - not a moment before you hurled them into eternity. The law is more merciful to you, because you will be afforded some period in which to make your peace with your Maker.*

Then donning the black cap, he continued:

> *I now pass upon you the dreadful sentence and judgment of this court - that is that you, William Smiley, be taken from this court to the prison from whence you came, and that on Wednesday, August 8, you be taken to the common place of execution in the jail in which you will have been confined, and then and there be hanged by the neck until you are dead, and that your body be buried within the walls of the prison. And may the Lord Almighty have mercy on your soul.*

As Smiley turned to leave the dock, the crowded court (the majority of whom were women) stood to have a last look at the man destined for the gallows. Once in the condemned cell, Smiley admitted his guilt and, taking the judge's advice, prepared to meet his God. On the last day of the month, the Northern Ireland Cabinet approved the hanging, sealing his doom.

Smiley is said to have walked the short distance from the cell to the scaffold with a smile on his lips. A crowd had began gathering outside the prison from about 7am but quickly and quietly dispersed after the official notices confirming that the death sentence had been carried out were posted on the jail door. The inquest, held in the prison at 10am by the city coroner, concluded: "Smiley had been duly executed by being hanged by the neck until dead, as required by law."

CHAPTER ELEVEN

THE BLOODY THIRTIES

I think that human beings who are not infallible ought not to choose a form of punishment which is irreparable.

Lord Chancellor Lord Gardiner

(during 1969 Lords debate on hanging)

The tightly-knit community of Toomebridge were
shocked by the murder of the village postman
(Ulster Museum).

Execution of Samuel Cushnan
8th April, 1930

AS POSTMAN James McCann cycled away from Toomebridge Post Office at 8.20am on 16th May, 1929, there could have been no inkling of what lay ahead. It was the 25-year-old's usual run, carrying letters to the rural community in and around the road to Crosskeys, some four miles away. This being a Thursday, he also had a sealed bag containing the old-age pension money for the district. The journey normally took little more than an hour, so by 10am he was already 30 minutes overdue and along his route people were becoming concerned that the postie hadn't been seen. Some 15 minutes later James McCann's body was found lying in a pool of blood in a quiet, lonely walkway known as Harris' Lane. He had been shot in the neck at close range, with 12 shotgun pellets later removed from the body. All around him were scattered the letters from his bag and the pension money was missing.

Within hours of the shooting a huge crowd had gathered at the top of the lane, all hoping to catch a glimpse of the body and murder scene. The local RUC, aided by detectives brought in from Belfast, began their investigation while forensic experts scarred the area for clues. Soon a picture began to be formed of the killing. A postmortem examination had revealed that Mr McCann had consumed a fair amount of alcohol shortly before his death, while a porter bottle half-full of poteen had been found in a hedge a short distance away. The postman, it seemed, had been lured up the laneway by a "callous, treacherous acquaintance, if not a friend". There were also reports of a farm worker named Samuel Cushnan being seen in the area shortly after the shooting. A piece of cloth found on a tree near the body was also identified as the same material as a coat Cushnan was known to wear everyday.

Cushnan was arrested and came to trial at the Ulster Winter Assizes in Londonderry in December, 1929. But, after four days of evidence, the jury failed to agree on a verdict and a retrial was ordered at the County Antrim Spring Assizes, beginning on 5th March, 1930. It also lasted four days, with the jurors locked up in the courthouse each evening. They were allowed, however, to go for a walk in the prison garden in the mornings before the court opened. Hundreds of spectators turned up on each day of the trial, thought most had to be content with milling about outside as the courtroom could not accommodate everyone.

**Postman James McCann was shot dead
in a quiet country lane at Crosskeys.**

Like most murder trials, the evidence was principally circumstantial. It was also generally weak. Two girls, for example, had seen a bike which looked like Cushnan's hidden in bushes at the end of Harris' Lane only hours after the murder. The bike, it was claimed, had been left there to aid escape, but the killer had panicked and made his getaway across the fields instead to the Toomebridge Road. The girls, however, were unable to positively identify it as belonging to the accused man. Likewise, the scrap of material found at the scene could be tied to him by the tailors Crawford and Barclay, of Ballymena, who had used their only three-and-a-half yards of that particular cloth to make up a suit for a Mr Cushnan in April, 1925. They could not rule out, however, that other companies in the district had not similarly bought quantities of the same fabric.

But as with Pratley some six years earlier, it was a letter written in prison which was to prove the most damaging to Cushnan. Meant for his brother Patrick, it read:

> Dear Brother Pat,
>
> I got the opportunity to drop you a line through the underground post. This letter will be posted by a trustworthy friend. If you get the scythe which I had mentioned on your last visit please let me know by putting three crosses in your next letter. Brother, the boy that will post this letter will give you a call in a day or two, so he is all right. If you like he will give you a hand to look for it. The name is James Kennedy. He will tell you a good plan to do with the scythe. As regards the money, you can remove it to a safer place if you think it is not safe where it is.

The murder weapon had not been found by the police. However, a search of Cushnan's home had turned up the stock of a shotgun bought by him in John Irwin's, Ballymena. The barrel was missing, allegedly stolen. It was this barrel that the "scythe" in the letter referred to, while the "money" was the pension cash, claimed the prosecution.

Cushnan, who was in the witness box for more than three hours, claimed he had spent the entire morning of the murder working in his potato plot. Described by his own counsel as a "gullible gulpin from Ballyscullion Bog," he was continuously urged to speak up while giving his evidence. Quizzed about the letter, Cushnan said the scythe referred to was an old rusty gun, hence the name. It belonged to his brother, and he had been advised by his cell mates that it should be produced to the police. The money was cash earned from the sale of livestock, which was to go to his solicitor towards the cost of his defence.

CUSHNAN'S FATE.

Toomebridge Crime Expiated in Belfast.

At eight o'clock yesterday morning Samuel Cushnan paid the penalty of the law at Belfast Prison for the murder fo James M'Cann, a rural postman, near Toomebridge, on May 16th, 1929. Pierpont was the executioner.

Large numbers of people assembled outside the prison in the drizzling rain, and some women repeated the Rosary at the hour fixed for the execution. Shortly after eight o'clock a notice, signed by Mr. J. Bristow, Sub-Sheriff, and Major A. W. Long, the prison governor, notifying that the sentence of the law had been carried out, was affixed to the prison gate by a warder.

An inquest was held in the prison at ten o'clock by Dr. James Graham, J.P., City Coroner. Dr. P. E. O'Flaherty, visiting medical officer to the prison, certified the cause of death, and, other evidence having been given, the Coroner returned a verdict of death by hanging, and expressed sympathy with the relatives.

Cushnan's fate, as the Belfast News Letter termed it, merited little column space, though a large crowd gathered outside the jail for the execution.

Lord Chief Justice William Moore, who donned
the black cap to sentence Cushnan to death,
at the opening of the assizes.

The jury, no doubt boosted by the Lord Chief Justice the Rt Hon William Moore's parting words of "and now, gentlemen, may God's blessing rest on your labours, and may you do your best in accordance with your oaths," took exactly 60 minutes to reach a verdict of guilty. Cushnan, "a short blue-coated figure standing immobile between two tall warders," listened impassively, his hands clasped in front of him, to the death sentence being read out before turning on his heels and leaving the dock.

The Northern Ireland Cabinet met on 31st March and confirmed the death sentence. However, there must have been misgivings for special meetings were convened on the 4th and 6th April to discuss the issue again, but without producing any change of heart. Tuesday, 8th April, dawned on a wet and miserable day, a light drizzle falling on the large crowd which had gathered outside the prison. As 8am neared, some of the women began reciting the Rosary while inside executioner Pierrepoint completed his preparations. Within seconds of the appointed hour, his work was done and Samuel Cushnan's body hung inert from the end of the gallows' rope. The inquest, held at 10 o'clock, expressed its sympathy to the relatives of the dead.

Execution of Thomas Dornan
31st July, 1931

THE ACT of murder is generally a private affair; an event carried out behind closed doors or on isolated laneways, well away from the public gaze. On the odd occasion that the foul deed has been perpetrated in front of others, the killer has usually made a determined attempt to escape. Thomas Dornan was an exception. After shooting dead two sisters, the second such double tragedy to come to north Antrim in less than three years, he simply strode off to his home to await the arrival of the police.

Dornan was a farmer who worked a small plot of land at Skerry East, about 12 miles north-east of Ballymena. He was, or at least had been, a respectable citizen in every way, serving as sexton of nearby Newtowncrommelin Presbyterian Church. But in December, 1929, the tongues began to wag after a local girl give birth to an illegitimate child. In due course the scandalmongers were rewarded when the girl, 18-year-old Bella Aiken, accused Dornan, who was twice her age, of being the father. To his credit, he admitted the child was his and agreed to pay Bella six shillings a week in maintenance.

But Dornan, despite his apparent good grace, was far from happy, though it was to take a further 17 months before his anger manifested itself in an orgy of hate. Early on the afternoon of 22 May, 1931, Dornan had seemed in good spirits as he walked among workers cutting peat from a bog near his home. He passed the time of day with some, but not Bella, who was toiling alongside her sister, Margaret, eight years her senior. The Aikens were, as the newspapers of the day put it, "of the labouring class," and worked in the bog to supplement their meagre existence. About half-an-hour later Dornan returned to the field, this time with a gun in his hand and apparently looking for something. He approached one of the workers, John McBurney, and asked: "Did you see any word of a white cat anywhere about?". He then went over to Bella, Margaret and another woman, Maud McCarthy, telling the last named that the "peats were not ready for castling". Taking a few more steps, Dornan stopped again and, raising the gun to his shoulder, fired at a startled Bella, hitting her in the arm. A second shot followed, and the girl threw herself across Margaret in desperation. Both women, screaming and crying, tried to get away across the field, but Dornan kept walking after them, reloading and firing. In total he discharged at least six shots.

While everyone else scattered, James Aiken, the women's brother, came running over to see what was going on and watched in horror as Dornan fired again into the now still

Double murderer Thomas Dornan was a
respected member of his community and had
served as sexton of Newtowncrommelin
Presbyterian Church.

bodies lying in a pool of blood on top of the peat. Stopped in his tracks, James challenged
Dornan, who responded by reloading his gun as if to fire on him. The young man ran off
home, a distance of about a quarter-mile, to raise the alarm. Dornan, meanwhile, walked
home where a neighbour, William Kelly, found him sitting at the kitchen table staring into
space.

On Wednesday, 8th July, Dornan appeared in the dock of Crumlin Road Courthouse
before the Lord Chief Justice. As in the previous County Antrim double killing, he was
only charged with one murder, that of Bella. Given the strength of the evidence, the only
worthwhile debate could be the question of his sanity, with medical experts giving
conflicting evidence. The jury took just 30 minutes to reach its verdict of guilty. Asked if
he had anything to say before sentence was passed, Dornan simply stared vacantly in front
of him. His trial had been the first held in Northern Ireland involving a capital offence
since the creation of the Court of Criminal Appeal in April, 1931. No appeal, however,
was lodged against the verdict.

**The Aiken family home at Skerry East, to where
James Aiken ran to raise the alarm.**

Only a handful of people turned up outside the jail on the day of execution, 31st July, 1931. Inside, Dornan was going through his final preparations after apparently enjoying a good night's sleep. On the previous day he had received his last visit from his wife Elizabeth and several other relatives, and had assured them he was prepared to meet his fate. This resolution stayed with him in his final hours and he walked calmly to his spot under the noose for executioner Pierrepoint to quickly despatch him.

Thomas Dornan, the inquest was later told, went to the scaffold with a smile on his face. "He died happy, of that I have no doubt," the acting Presbyterian chaplain, the Rev S Simms, was able to say.

Eddie Cullens being driven from a shed alongside
the Liverpool ferry after being returned to
Northern Ireland to stand trial.

Execution of Eddie Cullens
13th January, 1932

ON A FRIDAY night in September, 1931, a circular was issued to police stations throughout Northern Ireland. It marked the widening of the net in one of the most bizarre murders ever committed in the Province. Another 19 days were to pass before an arrest was made, and only then after an investigation which spanned Carrickfergus, Belfast, Liverpool, Leeds and London. The notice, released some 12 hours after the discovery of a body, read:

> *At 9am on 4th September, 1931, the body of an unknown man was found lying in a field at Seskin, West Division, Carrickfergus. The body was naked save for a lady's blue and white rubber cap, and the man appeared to have been dead about twelve hours. There were no signs of a struggle having taken place, and it is possible that the body may have been brought from a distance. There were two small wounds, believed to be gunshot wounds, one on the right temple, the other immediately below the right eye.*
>
> *Description - age about 35 years, height 6 feet 2 inches, clean shaven, black hair, brown eyes, high cheek bones; Roman nose, slightly turned to the right; large mouth, thick lips; very irregular teeth; slight burn-mark about two inches under the left ear; very dark, swarthy skin, muscular build; somewhat flat feet. The man is of Jewish or foreign appearance. The police are anxious to receive information respecting any man answering to the description who is missing, and will be grateful to anyone reporting the finding of any clothing.*

The body had been discovered by a young farm labourer, James McCalmont, from Milvarn, Ballyclare, who was out collecting milk that Thursday morning as usual when his horse began shying and refused to go any further. Looking over the dry stone wall he spotted the partially concealed corpse, which he promptly reported to his employer, farmer John Hall, who in turn notified the police.

Two days later, on the Saturday, an inquest was convened in Carrickfergus Courthouse. Its first task was to give permission for a postmortem examination to be carried out, which was performed while preliminary evidence was heard. The doctors found the man

Eddie Cullens, the only Jew to be executed at Belfast, and his Turkish victim Achmet Musa.

had been shot once, the bullet entering the skull half-an-inch in front of the right ear, passing through the brain before striking the back of the head and causing a fracture. It had then ricochetted, almost certainly causing the wound below the right eye. A bullet was also produced at the inquest by a police constable, who had found it in "some matter" lying on the operating table after the doctors had left! The murder weapon was later discovered to be a Walther 6.35mm gun. Meanwhile, the police appeal for reports of clothes being found was quickly rewarded. A bundle of items, found in a gateway at Church Lane, central Belfast, the day after the body was discovered was handed in. It included a blue waterproof coat, jacket and trousers, all of which had been roughly cut up.

The following Tuesday, 8th September, the body was secretly buried in Belfast by the Jewish Burial Society on the assumption that the victim was a member of the Hebrew faith (it later transpired he was actually a Muslim). In the intervening days a stream of people who were missing relatives had viewed the body in a bid to determine its identity.

Without any hard evidence, and with apparently no progress being made by the Royal Ulster Constabulary, wild rumours began to circulate. There were claims the dead man was a sailor, from one of the many foreign ships which called at Belfast, who had run foul of a shipmate and paid the price; others had him as one of a gang who had pulled off a series of spectacular robberies in Scotland and who had come across to Ulster to allow the heat to die down, only to have a falling out among thieves; while the more off-beat suggested the victim could be a Russian Jew who had been hunted down by Soviet agents. The truth, as is so often the case, turned out to be stranger than fiction, though it wasn't until the end of September, and following the detention of a man in Gerald Road police station, London, that the tale could be told.

The arrested man was a 28-year-old Cypriot-born American citizen named Eddie Cullens. There was now also a name for the body - Achmet Musa, a Turk. The two men had been part of sideshow act which also included two more Turks, Zaro Agha, claimed to be the oldest man in the world at 156, and Assim Redven. Together they arrived in England in April, 1931, joining the Bertram Mills' Circus the following month on its tour of the provincial towns. In August the circus arrived in Wavertree, a surburb of Liverpool, where Cullens hired a furnished house and lock-up garage under an assumed name. It was to be later claimed in court that Cullens' intention had been to murder Musa and bury him under the garage floor. This scheme, however, came unstuck because the property owner paid too much attention to his activities.

On 28th August, 1931, Cullens and Musa travelled to Belfast on the Liverpool ferry, having borrowed a car from Redven for the trip. Arriving next morning, they soon found accommodation at a boarding house on Donegall Quay run by a Mr and Mrs Ryan. Despite being an odd couple, the showmen appeared determined to enjoy themselves in a packed few days in Ireland. Musa, tall and well-built, was a married man with a wife and 15-year-old son back in Turkey. A former soldier who saw action during the First World War, he was said to be a considerable womaniser despite barely speaking a word of English. Cullens, on the other hand, was short and stocky. He had spent much of his younger days in Turkey before moving to America when he was 16. He lived in New York for five years, working as a film projectionist. A smart dresser, he was also, it appears, something of a ladies' man.

On the Saturday afternoon, only hours after arriving in Belfast, they met a girl named Rose McGoldrick outside the Great Northern Railway station in the city centre. After chatting to her for a while, they left her home, arranging to meet again outside the GPO. The next day the pair took Rose and a friend, Peggy Murphy, to Bangor for the day. On the way Cullens, who was himself Jewish, joked about trying to get Musa to pay for tea "but he was like a Jew and would not part with his money". More importantly, Rose was later to claim in court that at one point during the day a woman's blue and white bathing cap, similar to that found on Musa's corpse, had fallen out of the car's glove compartment. It was quickly put back by Cullens.

On the Monday, the two men took Rose to Londonderry, but left again without her after she failed to arrive at the rendezvous point on time. The pair spent most of the next day away as well, returning to the boarding house about 6pm. Later that evening Cullens offered to take the Ryans for a spin in the car, but was involved in a collision with a tram and had to leave the vehicle in for repair. On Wednesday, 2nd September, Cullens and Musa left the Ryans' house for the last time. They gave Matthew Ryan a lift into town - he was on his way to Celtic Park for the greyhound racing - dropping him off at the Albert Clock before driving up Corporation Street.

Twenty-four hours later, Cullens arrived at the Belfast to Liverpool ferry terminal alone. What exactly had happened in the meantime will never be known. Back in England, Cullens told his circus colleagues, who by then were in Leeds, that Musa had met a rich woman in Londonderry and was having a great time in Ireland. He even claimed

The crowd strains to catch a glimpse of Cullens
as he makes his first court appearance at
Carrickfergus to be charged with murder.

to have received a postcard from the dead Turk. The illusion was cruelly shattered, however, with the arrival of two CID officers from Belfast armed with a picture of Musa taken after death.

Cullens was tried at the Ulster Winter Assizes, held at Armagh, in December, 1931, before the Lord Chief Justice. The cost of his defence was partially met by contributions from the Province's Jewish community. The jury was told that Musa's body had been dropped into the field where it was found, probably being rolled off a two-and-a-half foot high wall which ran alongside the road. There was no evidence of a struggle or of the grass being trodden in the field, though a storm which had raged on the night of 2nd September would probably have removed such tell-tale signs.

Damning evidence came from James Hagan, who lived at Straidnahanna, two miles from Carrickfergus. He had been returning home late on 2nd September when he came across an Essex saloon car, similar to the one on loan to Cullens, stopped in a narrow roadway about midnight. Its sidelights were on and the driver, whom he later identified as the prisoner in the dock, claimed to be lost. Cullens, he said, asked him if he had room to get past and if he was on the right road to Larne. The crucial element of Mr Hagan's evidence was that it put Cullens, alone in the Essex car, less than a mile-and-a-half from the spot where Musa's body was found some 36 hours later.

Cullens, when he took the witness stand, insisted he had went into Celtic Park with Matthew Ryan, leaving Musa in the car. When they returned he had gone, he said. Cullens maintained that he had then returned with his landlord to the boarding house, where he spent the night. His story was flatly denied by Mr Ryan, who also alleged that Assim Redven had tried to bribe him into confirming Cullens' story when the Turk had visited the boarding house on 4th November. After three days of evidence, the jury retired for just 34 minutes before returning with a guilty verdict. Asked if he had anything to say why sentence should not be passed, Cullens replied: "All I can say is that when I swore on my oath yesterday that I was not guilty it was the Gospel truth," which is surely an odd turn of phrase for a Jew. The execution date was set for 29th December. That morning, however, rather than hanging from a rope in Belfast jail, Cullens was back in court "looking in the best of health" for the opening of his appeal hearing, the first time the Criminal Appeal Act had been enacted. It was a short respite, as his appeal was dismissed and an application to the Attorney General for a certificate to carry on to the House of Lords was similarly turned down. A revised date of 13th January, 1932, for the hanging remained unaltered.

Cullens last days were spent writing letters to his family of three sisters and a brother spread across Palestine, San Francisco and New York. Throughout his imprisonment he was visited regularly by Rabbi Shachter, head of the Jewish community in Ulster, who defied medical advice to stay with him to the end. After the execution he told a reporter:

> *The bravery of Cullens in meeting his fate was quite beyond the imagination. Up to five minutes before his death he was busy writing notes conveying his wishes and farewells to his relatives. It was with a smiling face that he parted with everyone, repeating again and again to me that he was going to face his Maker with the full satisfaction that his hands were clean of the blood of the murdered man.*

Cullens was the only Jew hanged at Belfast and possibly in Ireland as a whole. The case left many questions unanswered, including the vexed notion of a motive, though there was speculation, fueled by Cullens in his appeal, that others were involved in the plot. On the practical side, it has to be asked how a small, dapper man like Cullens managed to lift the body of Musa, 6ft 2ins tall and weighing 14 stone, over the wall into the field without help? And, of course, why did the corpse have a bathing cap on its head? It is unlikely we will ever know with any degree of certainty.

Telegraphic Address : " Homaff " Belfast.
Telephone No.—Belfast 8321.
   Any reply to this communication should
be addressed :
Secretary,
   Ministry of Home Affairs,
      Stormont, Belfast,
         Northern Ireland,
and the following reference number quoted—
Ref. No. .................M.S.3471................

Ministry of Home Affairs,
Stormont,
Belfast,
Northern Ireland.
5th April, 1933.

Sir,

          I am directed to inform you that petitions on
behalf of HAROLD COURTNEY, a prisoner in Belfast
Prison under sentence of death, have been duly
considered by the Cabinet, who have failed to
discover any grounds which would justify them in
advising His Grace the Governor of Northern Ireland
to interfere with the due course of law.

          His Grace has, accordingly, decided that the
law must take its course.

                    I am, Sir,
                    Your obedient Servant,

                    Lamahll

                    Asst., SECRETARY.

Valentine Wilson, Esq.,
     Under Sheriff for County Armagh,
     ARMAGH.

LW.

All hope for Harold Courtney was lost
when the Stormont Cabinet decided against
advising the Governor to grant a reprieve
(Public Record Office).

Execution of Harold Courtney
7th April, 1933

MINNIE REID adjusted her hat and pulled on her overcoat, struggling to button it across her ever increasing bulge. It wouldn't be long now, she thought, before the baby was to be born. And just as certainly, she knew, she was soon to lose her refuge at the Portadown home of David Collen. The Collens had already decided to close up the house on Stewart Avenue, leaving Minnie with neither a job nor a place to stay. The problem was weighing heavily on her mind on that July night in 1932. Without a husband to explain her condition, she was too scared and ashamed to return to her parents. Picking up the tray holding her master's supper, Minnie left the scullery and made her way to the living quarters. Although it was an hour earlier than the usual meal time, the Collens made no comment for it was obvious the housemaid intended heading out that night. Within minutes she was gone, never to be seen alive again.

A week later, Minnie Reid's body was found among thick laurels in the grounds of the Vernersbridge estate, close to Symington's Lane and about eight miles away from the Collen house. Her throat had been cut, leaving a gaping five inch wound, and her clothes and the surrounding ground were thickly covered in congealed blood. The body was lying on its back, with the clothes and feet drawn up, though there was no sign of sexual assault. Indeed, there was no true evidence that she had even been murdered, as opposed to having taken her own life. Several days after the body was found, and following the pain-staking clearance of the bushes by the police, a blood-stained razor was found some 13 feet away from where the corpse had lay.

From the police investigation which followed, there emerged a prime suspect by the name of Harold Courtney, a 23-year-old driver from Dungannon. Courtney was something of a ladies' man, always carrying on in their presence and running around with a host of different girls. His friendship with Minnie went back a long way, and had included finding her a job in Langland's Hotel, literally on his own doorstep in Dungannon. Letters found in Minnie's room after she died showed the pair had been writing to one another for some time and had arranged to meet on several occasions. Yet, when initially interviewed by the RUC, Courtney denied having anything beyond a passing acquaintence with the girl. When eventually arrested he admitted telling lies, claiming he wanted to distance himself from Minnie as he was engaged to be married to Lonie Motum from Dunmurry, who was the "jealous type". Indeed, the pair were to have wed on 21st September, 1932, less than two months after Minnie's death.

The jury were unable to agree a verdict at Courtney's first trial at Downpatrick in December, and so the final scene came to be played out at Armagh Courthouse in March, 1933. There was still the crucial question to be answered: had a murder been committed or was Minnie Reid's death suicide. Each side called two eminent doctors, who took fundamentally opposing views. For the Crown, pathologist Prof John Young and Dr George Dougan conceded it might have been suicide but considered it more likely to have been murder. Likewise for the defence, Belfast surgeon T S Kirk and Dr M T Whitla, from Monaghan, admitted the wound could have been caused by an assailant, but thought it more likely the girl had taken her own life. The strongest point in the suicide theory was the fact that Minnie would not have lost consciousness for several minutes after the wound had been inflicted, yet had made no effort to move or get up, but had simply sat there waiting for death.

Despite the conflicting evidence, the Attorney-General entertained no such doubts. He told the court: "I say that the prisoner, and the prisoner alone, stands in the centre of the evidence and that every thread leads directly to him; I say it is as clear as a sign-post on a main road; I say no other person could fill the position as prisoner does."

Courtney, the court was told, had in all probability fathered the child Minnie had been expecting and had wanted to silence her. While the evidence against him was circumstantial, it quickly mounted up. A park keeper claimed he had seen the pair together at Donaghmore in June, 1932; a taxi driver told the court he had taken a woman answering Minnie's description to Verner's estate on 25th July to meet someone; a railway porter said Courtney had called at Vernersbridge station on 26th July looking to meet someone off the train.

On the night of Minnie's disappearance, Courtney had hired a car from Robert Ardery, driving off in it at 8pm and returning about 10.15pm. He claimed to have used it to go to Armagh in search of a man who had offered him a better paid job. However, 13-year-old Olive Symington reported seeing a similar car parked in a laneway close to the murder scene about 9pm that evening. After five days of evidence, the jury retired for little more than an hour before returning to the courtroom. The Belfast News Letter reported:

> Courtney retained his composure to the end. Anxiety, however, was clearly written on his countenance as the jury slowly filed back into court after an hour and a quarter of deliberation. The ashen grey of the faces of some of them indicated to the observant the momentous decision at which they had arrived. The prisoner stood between warders in the dock, raising and lowering himself ever so slightly on his toes, his chest rising and falling with emotion. It was his first outward sign of anxiety in the five days.

Along with the guilty verdict, the jury included a strong recommendation for mercy. Any hope that might have aroused in Courtney was quickly dispersed by the Lord Chief Justice, however, who told the prisoner:

Harold Courtney, a jury of your fellow countrymen have brought in a verdict with which I cordially agree, and every reasonably thinking man in the court would, I think, arrive at the same conclusion. It is my duty out of respect to the jury to forward their recommendation of mercy to the proper authorities, but in doing so it is only fair that I should tell you that I profoundly disagree with it. I think it was a cold blooded, calculated and callous murder. I think you betrayed this girl; under the stress of her claims upon you, you butchered her and her unborn child. I may tell you - it is only fair to tell you - that so far as I am concerned I can hold out no hope that the sentence will not be carried out.

The execution date was set for Friday, 7th April, 1932, and remained unchanged. A crowd began gathering outside the prison gates from early on, eventually growing large enough to block traffic for a while. A few seconds after 8am, Pierrepoint, the executioner, pushed the lever and Harold Courtney dropped to his death. Two hours later the formalities were completed when the inquest returned a verdict of lawful execution and Courtney's remains joined those of the other murderers who had breathed their last in the jail.

The execution of Courtney was the second overseen by Prison Governor Capt Thomas Moore Stuart. He was also in charge when Eddie Cullens and Tom Williams were hanged (Public Record Office).

MYSTERY OF AN ULSTER GIRL'S DEATH

BODY IN LONELY LANE

Gruesome Discovery by Boys While at Play

MURDER SUSPECTED

Mystery surrounds the death of a girl of 22 years whose body was found at The Birches, between Portadown and Dungannon, yesterday, with her throat cut. The body had apparently been lying in a little-frequented lane for some days, and the theory held at present is that the girl was murdered.

The dead girl was Minnie Reid, of Drain, Eglish, near Dungannon, and she had been employed in Portadown as a domestic servant.

The body was found at a place called Derryane. A number of boys were playing in the laneway, which is near Milltown Retcory, on Tuesday, and they noticed a girl lying—as they thought—asleep. She was partly covered with bracken, and the boys did not look at her closely.

Yesterday, however, one of the boys again visited the lane, and when he saw that the girl was in the same place he guessed that something was wrong, and reported the matter to the Birches police.

GLOVE STUFFED IN WOUND

Sergeant Smith proceeded to the place, and Dr. George Dangan, Portadown, was summoned to make an examination of the body. The girl's throat had been badly gashed, and a glove was stuffed tightly in the wound. The medical opinion was that the body had been in the same place for about ten days, but a friend of the girl in Dungannon received a letter from her last Friday, so that it is thought her death may have been more recent.

NO INSTRUMENT FOUND

No instrument was found with which the wound could have been inflicted, and this lends strength to the theory that a murder has been committed.

In the girl's handbag was found a postcard addressed to herself, and letters giving her Portadown address.

Head-Constable Gosnell and Sergeant Stafford, Portadown, also inspected the place where the body was found, and subsequently investigations were made by County-Inspector Dudgeon, and Head-Constables Slacke and Brown, Belfast.

The dead girl was a daughter of Mr. and Mrs. Robert Reid, of Eglish. For some years she was employed as a domestic servant by Mrs. Hale, Fairview, Dungannon, and subsequently by Mrs. S. Langlands, Beaconsfield House, Dungannon. On July 12th she left to take up work with Mrs. Collen, of Stanford Avenue, Portadown.

LETTER TO A FRIEND

On Friday last Miss Lily Kelly, Ranfurly Avenue, Dungannon, a friend of the dead girl, received from her a letter in which she said she expected to have a few days' holiday, as her mistress was to go to the Dublin Show.

Mrs. Langlands, who was distressed when she heard of the girl's death, spoke very highly of her, and said she was a quiet girl who was popular with all her friends.

The news of the death of their daughter was broken to Mr. and Mrs. Reid by the police, and they received a terrible shock. Deep sympathy is felt for them throughout the district.

The Belfast News Letter report of the discovery of pregnant Minnie Reid's body on 3rd August, 1932

CHAPTER TWELVE

FOR THE SAKE OF IRELAND

*Many of us remember the time, not all
that long ago, when human life was prized
in this land and when a murder was talked
about, in horror, for months*

**Former Presbyterian Moderator
Dr John Dunlop**

(at the 1992 funeral of a murdered RUC officer)

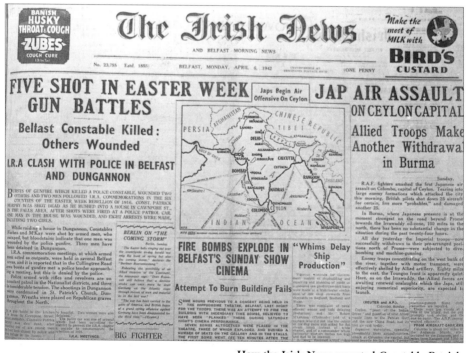

How the Irish News reported Constable Patrick
Murphy's murder and the arrest of the IRA gang.

Execution of Thomas Williams
2nd September, 1942

GIVEN Northern Ireland's troubled history, it is perhaps surprising that only one terrorist has been hanged on the Belfast gallows. That dubious distinction fell to Thomas Joseph Williams, who was executed in Crumlin Road Jail on 2nd September, 1942. If events had taken a different course, however, he could have been one of six IRA men to die that day.

The IRA had been quick to seize the opportunity the Second World War presented to mount its own campaign aimed at forcing the British out of Ireland. Indeed, on the day war was declared there were several incidents, including shots fired at the police. It was to England, however, that the IRA turned its attentions first. A plan had been drawn up to mount a bombing campaign on the mainland. No loss of life was envisaged, rather the intention was to make the English realise the potential trouble the Irish terror group posed in the hope it would shake their resolve to maintain the Union. It was an ill-conceived and even naive policy which went tragically wrong when five people were killed in a bomb attack for which two IRA men, Peter Barnes and Frank Richards, alias McCormick, were later executed.

South of the Irish border, the police took a stong line with the IRA, verging on a personal grudge between the two organisations. Casualties mounted up on both sides, and a number of terrorists paid the price on the gallows. In Northern Ireland, despite isolated incidents, the IRA showed little sense of purpose in the early war years. This, in no small measure, had been due to the success of the RUC in arresting suspects in swoops prior to the outbreak of hostilities with Germany. However, in 1942 the IRA's Northern Command decided to mount a campaign of its own which was ultimately to claim the lives of five RUC and Special Constabulary members and resulted in the deaths of three terrorists, including Tom Williams.

About 3pm on Easter Sunday, 1942, a four-man RUC patrol slowly drove up Clonard Gardens in Belfast, heading towards Cupar Street. As the vehicle reached the Kashmir Road junction a fusillade of shots rang out, between seven and 10 rounds in total, fired by a group of five men who had been hiding behind an air raid shelter. Only one bullet struck the car, smashing the windscreen but causing no injuries.

As the gang took off, three police officers leapt from the car and gave chase into Kashmir Road and down Cawnpore Street. A house to house search was started, during which Constable Patrick Murphy entered number 54 Cawnpore Street to be confronted

IRA man Tom Williams holds the double distinction of being the only terrorist executed within the jail and the only body for which permission has been granted for burial elsewhere (National Graves Association).

by the gunmen. In an exchange of shots, the officer fell fatally wounded, his service Webley revolver still clasped in his right hand. Shortly afterwards the police arrested six men and two girls in a bedroom of the house. One, Williams, was wounded with two bullets in his left thigh and one in his left arm, all fired by Constable Murphy. It later emerged the officer had fired only three rounds, each finding its target, before his gun misfired.

Constable Murphy, who had been stationed at Springfield Road barracks, had lived at Clowney Street, off the Falls Road. He left a widow and nine children. The RUC band led his funeral cortege from St Paul's Roman Catholic Church to Milltown cemetery, with 100 colleagues, including the City Commissioner and Deputy Commissioner in attendance. Two months later, during a three-day Royal visit to the Province, King George VI presented his widow with her husband's Police Medal during a special ceremony at Stormont Castle.

A few weeks later, on 28th July, 1942, the trial of the six men - Henry Cordner, William Perry, John Oliver, Patrick Simpson, Joseph Cahill and Williams - began before Lord Justice Murphy at the Belfast City Commission. All were aged between 18-21.

There was little doubt of their collective guilt in the incident, though obviously some bore more responsibility than others. In a lengthy statement, given eight days after the murder from his bed in the Royal Victoria Hospital, Williams claimed that he alone had organised the attack "as a protest against the English occupying Ireland". He had armed the men and been solely responsible for Constable Murphy's death, he said. It had been previously arranged, he told police, that after the shooting the weapons - a short Webley, three Webleys and a Parabellum - would be handed over to two girls and Simpson (who though he never had a gun was found with nine bullets in his pockets when arrested) in an entry off Cawnpore Street. The girls panicked, however, and followed the men into the house.

> I ran into the parlour and I heard the police knocking at the next door, the second one from Cupar Street. I then grabbed my revolver from the brown leather bag which was lying on the floor in the kitchen. This was the bag we put the revolvers into in the entry and was brought to the house by the girls. Some one of the eight persons said that a policeman was coming into the house by the entry door. I ran into the scullery. There is a little glass enclosure in the yard and from the scullery window I could see a policeman coming into this enclosure with his gun drawn.
>
> When he was about three yards from me and beside the kitchen window I pointed my revolver at his body and fired one shot. He staggered and fired back, and I fired four or five more shots at his body. The revolver I had was re-loaded by me after it had been brought to the house by the girls. No other person in the house had fired at Constable Murphy. I then shouted that I had been shot. I dropped my revolver and heard Constable Murphy groan and fall to the ground. Constable Murphy's body was lying between the glass enclosure and the door which leads from the scullery to the kitchen. I stepped over his body and ran into the hall of the house and there I fainted.
>
> Next thing I remember - when I woke up on a bed in the back room up the stairs - some of the party I had commanded said 'What do you want us to do?' I said 'Where are the police' and someone answered 'They have the house surrounded' and I told them to surrender, which they did. About five policemen came into the room where I was lying and they arrested us.

It was a gallant attempt by Williams - who described himself in a letter smuggled out of the jail as a lieutenant in C Company of the IRA's Belfast brigade - to give his accomplices a chance of escaping the gallows, and was never seriously challenged in court. Besides, as the law stood if one was guilty of murder, they all were, regardless of who pulled the trigger. However, Constable Murphy was shot five times, twice in the chest and

Veteran republican Joe Cahill, one of six men
sentenced to death for the murder of a
policeman, with Sinn Fein president Gerry Adams
at an anti-internment rally outside Belfast
City Hall, 1995 (Allan McCullough).

three times in the abdomen, with one bullet passing through his heart. A sixth bullet struck his gun holster. Robert Churchill, a London ballistics expert, said in evidence that four revolvers, including the constables, had been fired in the house. Const Murphy, he claimed, had three bullets in him from a Webley and two from a short Webley.

The Attorney General, in answering charges that Joe Cahill, who later went on to become the Provisional IRA's chief of staff in the early 1970s, had been severely assaulted by the arresting officers, told the court:

> *Even if, seeing his comrade lying in a pool of blood, some constable did not treat Cahill with gentle care, didn't that point in another direction from that indicated by learned counsel for the defence? Was it not a two-edged weapon? Didn't it indicate that the police regarded Cahill as being directly connected with what had happened downstairs in that house?*

The 12-strong jury, which had taken 90 minutes to select because of almost 150 challenges by both parties, retired on the third day. It returned after two hours and five minutes with six guilty verdicts, but with a recommendation for mercy in Simpson's case because of his youth. Williams last words to the court were: "I am not guilty of murder. I am not afraid to die. There was no premeditation." The execution date was set for 18th August, but was put back when appeal papers were lodged.

Within days 60,000 people in nationalist areas had signed a petition calling for a reprieve. Forms had been available in the porches of Roman Catholic churches on the Sunday following the verdict, and priests implored their congregations to sign them. Later that afternoon schools were opened up to act as centres for the collection of signatures. When the petition was finally handed in to the Stormont Minister of Home Affairs on 22nd August, it had almost 200,000 names on it.

Meanwhile, telegrams asking for support had been sent across the world to influencial people, including American President Franklin D Roosevelt, British Prime Minister Winston Churchill, Home Secretary Herbert Morrison and several Irish-American groups. Nationalist members of the Northern Ireland Parliament and Senate appealed directly to the Governor to save the men: "With a deep sense of our responsibility, we plead for mercy towards them," they wrote. "We submit to your judgment that the exercise of mercy would satisfy the ends of justice, and allay anxiety and apprehension agitating many minds about their fate."

South of the Irish border, a Dublin Reprieve Committee was formed and was widely supported by both the public and political figures. Taoiseach Eamonn De Valera met a number of delegations urging his support, including one from union leader James Larkin.

The Court of Appeal sat on Wednesday and Thursday, 19th and 20th August, 1942, the verdict that the convictions must stand being delivered the next day. A new date of 2nd September was fixed for the hangings. Leave to appeal to the House of Lords was lodged on 26th August but refused by the Attorney-General. The following day a conference in the Mansion House, Dublin, called on the people of Ireland to make the day of execution

Telegrams were sent to British Prime Minister Winston Churchill, seen here on a visit to Queen's University in Belfast in 1929, asking for mercy for the six condemned men (Public Record Office).

one of national mourning. The resolution said the conference "conscious of the deep feeling that the execution of any of the six men would arouse, urges the Irish people to show the utmost restraint, and to make it known to the world that any such execution had not the sanction of the Irish people".

The Northern Ireland Cabinet discussed the death sentences, and the possible unrest which would follow them, at length on 26th, 27th and 29th August. The next day, Sunday, 30th August, a statement was issued on behalf of the Governor. It read:

> *His Grace the Governor of Northern Ireland has considered the cases of Thomas Joseph Williams, William J Perry, Henry Cordner, John Terence Oliver, Joseph Cahill and Patrick Simpson, prisoners lying under sentence of death in H M Prison, Belfast, and has decided: That in the case of Thomas Joseph Williams the law must take its own course; That in the case of William J Perry, Henry Cordner, John T Oliver and Joseph Cahill sentence*

Taoiseach Eamonn De Valera received delegations, including one lead by union leader James Larkin, urging his help in having the sentences commuted (News Letter).

of death shall be commuted to one of penal servitude for life; and that in the case of Patrick Simpson sentence of death shall be commuted to penal servitude for 15 years.

The news was given to the men by their solicitor, with the others taking it in turn to embrace Williams, who apparently showed no emotion but told them: "Don't worry about me. I am all right. I am fully prepared to die." As word spread of the reprieves, cheering crowds gathered outside the homes of the men. Dublin's Lord Mayor, Alderman P S Doyle, arrived in Belfast the day after the Governor's statement and in the wake of a telegram sent to his Belfast counterpart which read:

Lord Mayor, City Hall, Belfast
  Corporation of Dublin in special meeting assembled unanimously adopted the following resolution: That the Corporation of the City of Dublin gives its fullest support to the appeal for the reprieve of the six young men awaiting execution in Belfast Jail. In view of the good relationship which exists between the two corporations, I earnestly request you to exercise your good offices in the matter.

Before treating Mr Doyle to lunch in the City Hall, followed by private meetings, the Belfast councillors had already formulated their reply:

> *Resolved: That this Council appreciate the reference to the good relationship existing between the two bodies and the motives which prompted the request but they feel that as the subject has already been dealt with by His Grace the Governor of Northern Ireland, action on their part is not called for.*

At 8am on 2nd September, 1942, 19-year-old Tom Williams walked the short distance from the condemned cell to the gallows at the beginning of a day of violence and protest throughout Ireland. The RUC were well aware of the risk of violence. Two days earlier another IRA man, moving arms in preparation for revenge attacks for Williams' execution, had been shot dead at Hannahstown. On the eve of the hanging, a crowd had gathered outside the jail, catching the police unaware. The following morning, in a bid to frustrate similar scenes, a large area around the prison was cordoned off, with patrol cars and tenders much in evidence on the streets. The Crumlin Road was closed from Carlisle Circus to Agnes Street, forcing vehicles and pedestrians to make diversions. Tramcars, carrying workers on their way to the mills and factories, were the only vehicles allowed past the prison, and only then on the condition they didn't stop. Those living in the restricted area could only pass the jail after producing their identity cards to police.

Inside the prison, Williams had celebrated Mass at 6.35am and again at 7.15am. He is said to have joined in the prayers as he was led to the scaffold by the prison chaplain, the Rev Patrick McAlister. The previous evening he had been visited by his brother Richard, who was serving with the Irish army's air corps, his elderly grandmother, Margaret Fay, with whom he had lived, and an uncle, Charles Fay. Williams also received a telegram from his father, serving in the Irish army. It read: "Be brave to the end, my son. Goodbye, and God bless you."

Several hundred people gathered on the pavement outside the cordon, with many of the women offering up prayers for the soul of the teenager. A rival faction had taken up position on the opposite side of the street, and as the appointed time of execution drew closer the tension threatened to spill over.

The Belfast News Letter reported:

> *Police had to intervene at the corner of Old Lodge Road and Florence Place, which runs alongside the County Courthouse. Here on the stroke of eight, a crowd of about 200 women and girls burst into 'God Save the King,' while on the other side of the street a score of women were kneeling. Cheers followed the National Anthem, and then the crowd sang 'Land of Hope and Glory' and 'There'll always be an England,' the praying women meanwhile remaining on their knees.*

A republican memorial in Milltown Cemetery, known as the old Fenian monument,
carries Tom Williams' name. Alongside it (out of camera shot) is the County Antrim monument,
where a grave had been reserved for the IRA man.

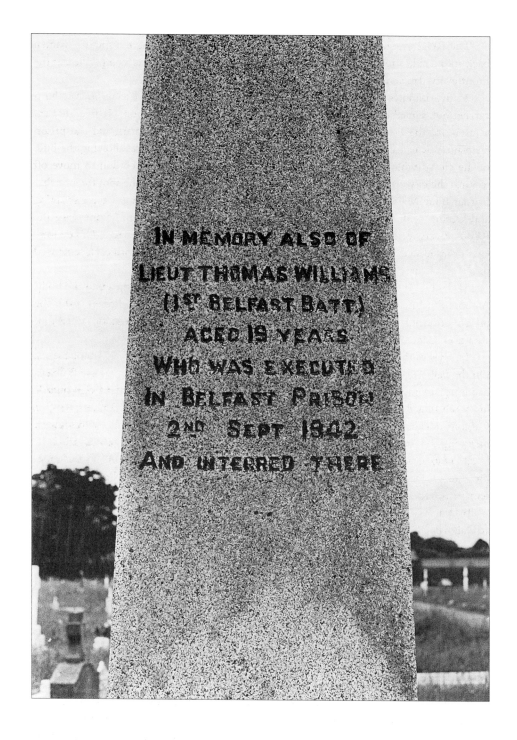

IN MEMORY ALSO OF
LIEUT THOMAS WILLIAMS
(1ST BELFAST BATT.)
AGED 19 YEARS
WHO WAS EXECUTED
IN BELFAST PRISON
2ND SEPT 1942
AND INTERRED THERE

The RUC eventually managed to restore order, gradually forcing the singing women back into a side street, with one woman calling out: "There are men being killed at the Front every day, and they don't pray for them."

At five minutes past eight o'clock the official notice that the execution had been carried out, signed by the Under-Sheriff of Belfast, Robert Henderson, George Stewart, a Justice of the Peace, prison governor Captain Thomas Moore Stuart, and the prison chaplain, was nailed to the jail's main door. The police then withdrew, allowing the bulk of the crowd which had gathered at the Carlisle Circus end of the cordon to move off towards the city centre. Some women remained, however, praying at the spot for a further half-an-hour. Marshalled by police, the protestors passed through Royal Avenue shouting and singing, with some giving Nazi salutes, and on to the Falls Road. At one stage the RUC officers were pelted with stones and bottles, and two men were arrested. They were later charged with striking a Head-Constable and riotous behaviour, with each sentenced to a total of three months imprisonment.

An inquest on Williams was opened at 11am, with all the jurors inspecting the body. A short funeral service, officiated by three priests, was held at noon. Present were the prison governor and a number of Roman Catholic warders, who stood rigidly to attention as the coffin was lowered into the ground.

The rest of the day was marked by protests and disturbances in Roman Catholic areas. On the Falls Road a flag-waving crowd marched down to Bombay Street, where Williams had lived, singing republican songs along the way. After holding a short silent vigil outside his home, they dispersed again. Elsewhere, black flags appeared in nationalist areas; Roman Catholic dockers in Belfast, Londonderry and Newry walked out; and police and soldiers, including the American forces, were insulted and occasionally attacked with missiles.

In Dublin, many businesses closed for an hour and flags were flown at half-mast. Protesters forced buses to turn back in the city centre and several of the shops which remained open, including Easons in Sackville Street, had their windows smashed.

Back in Northern Ireland, a car and lorry full of armed IRA men crossed the border at Culloville, Co Armagh, about 2.15pm that day. A police patrol, consisting of a sergeant and constable on Customs duty, spotted the truck and gave chase. As the RUC men rounded a corner they found their path blocked by the gang, which opened fire, riddling the car. The officers returned fire but were quickly overpowered. The sergeant and one of the raiders were slightly injured in the gun battle, which ended with the gang fleeing back across the border.

Williams dying wish, it was later claimed, was to be buried in the republican plot at Milltown cemetery and a campaign to have his body exhumed was soon underway. The National Graves Association, which registers and maintains republican burial plots, reserved a grave for Williams at the County Antrim monument in the cemetery and took legal action in a bid to force the Government to release the IRA man's remains. The courts, in a judicial review, ruled the Northern Ireland Secretary of State had the power to have commuted the part of the sentence which required the body to remain in an unmarked prison grave. A warrant removing this clause was signed by the Queen in

August, 1995, and the announcement that the body was to be exhumed made the following month, just days after the 53rd anniversary of Williams' execution.

Inside the jail, the grave site was located. Next to it, on the garden wall, was found scored into the brickwork the IRA man's initials, T W. However, a dispute between members of the Williams family and the National Graves Association over where he should be reburied delayed the release of the remains. At the time of writing, the Northern Ireland Office was seeking legal advice on its position while attempting to find a compromise through discussions with the parties involved.

CHAPTER THIRTEEN

THE CURTAIN DROPS

*In fifty years time this event will be
looked back on with the same attitude
that we now have to witch-hunting*

**Denis Barritt,
of the Society of Friends**

(after a Belfast execution in 1961)

Prison Governor Lance Thompson, seen here on his daily inspection tour of the jail with the head warder, was in charge during the last two executions in Belfast (Public Record Office).

Execution of Samuel McLaughlin
25th July, 1961

"I NEVER intended hurting or harming my wife. I always loved my wife," Samuel McLaughlin told a hushed courtroom moments before being sentenced to death for her murder. They were heartfelt words from a man who had quite literally destroyed his own world during a bout of jealous rage sparked by days of excessive drinking.

McLaughlin was normally a quiet, inoffensive man who had left his native Cloughmills, in County Antrim, in 1941, aged 21, to enlist in the RAF. He saw service in Belgium, France and Italy as the victorious Allied forces pressed through Europe on the heels of the retreating Germans. Once in Italy, however, his troubles began. Caught dealing on the black market, he was tried by court martial and sentenced to three years in jail, later reduced to two years. His time behind bars was served in England and he was discharged from the airforce on his release from prison in 1949.

Returning home again to Northern Ireland, his luck appeared to be changing as he quickly found work, driving a lorry, and romance. The latter came in the form of an old friend, Nellie Given, whom he had known as a child. Now, however, she was an attractive 21-year-old member of the Auxiliary Territorial Service. Their relationship blossomed, and in 1951 they married. The young couple moved to Derby, where McLaughlin had found a job in a foundry. Living at first in a furnished flat, they were finally allocated a council house. After a few years, however, McLaughlin moved to another factory, turning out parts for lawnmowers, and seemed well settled in his new surroundings. Nellie, on the other hand, was extremely unhappy. She detested their new house, didn't get on with the neighbours and felt desperately home-sick.

Eventually, at Christmas, 1959, Nellie could stick it no longer and moved back to stay with her mother in a two-roomed cottage at Lislaban, Cloughmills. McLaughlin, much to his disgust, was ordered to pay his wife £3 week in maintainence. At the hearing she accused him of ill-treatment and infidelity, while he countered by claiming she was "nagging and difficult".

Despite the accusations, McLaughlin still obviously loved his wife and she apparently still felt something for him. Nonetheless, as he was to tell police later, he believed she was "playing around" since their separation, possibly sparking the violence which was to follow.

A warder nails the notice to the prison door
confirming that Samuel McLaughlin had been
duly executed for the murder of his wife
(News Letter).

In October, 1960, he took time off from the Qualcast foundry and, having two days previously signed for a new house to which he hoped to bring back his 32-year-old wife, he headed off on his motorbike to catch the boat to Ulster. Once home, he spent the next few days calling on friends and drinking in the pubs. Strangely, it wasn't until Monday, 17th October, the day he had originally planned returning to Derby, that he met up with Nellie. The reunion evidently went well, with most of that evening spent together in Richmond's pub in Cloughmills. At one stage Nellie began singing "Goodnight Irene," into her husband's face, bringing tears to his eyes. Delicately she wiped them away as McLaughlin took up the song. The couple returned, armed with a carryout of stout, whiskey and rum, to the home Nellie shared with her mother, Martha Given, and continued their drinking. Later, in front of a blazing fire, they made love.

The following day, McLaughlin, Nellie and Mrs Given had lunch together before the couple set off on the motorbike to visit friends. That evening it was back to the pubs for another drinking bout. About 9pm they went for a meal, returned to the pub for a last drink, then headed off to the cottage around 10pm. That was the last time Nellie was seen alive.

That Tuesday night the pair had the cottage to themselves for Mrs Given, at Nellie's request, had went to stay with relatives. When she returned home about noon the following day she found the doors locked and the blinds drawn. Later, with still no life about the cottage, Nellie's half-sister Violet Houston alerted the police, who despatched Special Constable Norman McIntyre. The constable, using his torch, peered through a window and spotted a body lying on the bed. He sent for Dr David Johnston Crawford, who climbed into the house through a window. Inside, he found Nellie's partially clothed body covered in blood. She had been beaten repeatedly with a broom handle, the broken remains of which lay on the floor. Death, however, had been caused by strangulation, the white nylon stocking used still tightly wrapped around her throat.

McLaughlin, soon in police custody, maintained throughout that he had no recollection of how his wife came to die, while virtually admitting in the same breath that he had killed her. During his interviews with the RUC he appeared confused and disorientated. "If I tied that stocking round her neck I may or may not have done it. I just don't know how it was done or something," was a typical response from him when quizzed.

The case was heard at the Northern Ireland Winter Assizes in February, 1961, but the jury, after much wrestling with the laws covering insanity, failed to agree on a verdict. As a consequence, McLaughlin again found himself in the dock, this time during the County Antrim Spring Assizes in April that year. There could be little doubt he had killed his wife but there was considerable disagreement as to his state of mind. Evidence was given by a former RAF colleague that he was prone to acts of senseless violence and memory loss when on drinking binges, though binge seems barely adequate a word to describe his intake. Between 13th October and 18th October, 1960, McLaughlin was estimated to have consumed daily three dozen Guinness, a half-bottle of whiskey and a half-bottle of rum.

Dr John Nabney, a psychiatrist working at Purdysburn Hospital in Belfast, told the court that McLaughlin's first recollection on the day following the murder had been of finding himself up a grass lane "looking for a tree to hang himself". He was aware something terrible had happened but did not know his wife was dead, it was said. It was not a tree, however, but the gallows inside Crumlin Road Jail which was selected for the hanging when the jury returned with a guilty verdict after two hours and 20 minutes of deliberations. The execution date was set for 17th May, but had to be postponed after an appeal was lodged. The four-day hearing in the Court of Appeal, at the end of June, confirmed the original sentence and a new date was set.

On the morning of 25th July, 1961, 40-year-old Samuel McLaughlin joined his wife in the hereafter. The Rev A S Hoffmeester, who as curate of St Mary's Church of Ireland on the Crumlin Road acted as prison chaplain and attended McLaughlin throughout his last hours, rarely discusses the experience and declined to be interviewed for this book. However, he once admitted that to prepare himself for the traumatic ordeal, he had to ask a local hospital for tranquillisers, an indication of just how difficult it was for everyone associated with a hanging.

At 8.10am, a notice confirming the execution had taken place was nailed to the jail door. The heavy police presence, which included patrol cars, comfortably dealt with the 100 or so people who had gathered outside the gates of the courthouse opposite. When they surged forward, on seeing the notice posted, they were stopped in their tracks by an RUC cordon. Denis Barritt, a member of the Society of Friends and ardent opponent of capital punishment, told a reporter outside the gates: "In fifty years time this event will be looked back on with the same attitude that we now have to witch-hunting. Hanging is a terrible, uncivilised thing." The crowd dispersed quietly after 10 minutes when a head-constable ordered them to move on. By the time executioner Harry Allan left the jail, some two hours later, it was business as usual on the Crumlin Road.

Execution of Robert McGladdery
20th December, 1961

A SINGLE black shoe lay in the middle of the road. Not in itself a remarkable happening, but strange enough to cause Charles Ashe to stop and ponder. The 16-year-old was out early that Saturday morning, 28th January, 1961, exercising greyhounds when he came across the shoe lying on the Old Damolly Road, outside Newry. Picking it up, Charles examined it briefly before tossing it aside into the hedges. Carrying on towards Damolly crossroads, however, he came across other, more mystifying objects: a silk scarf in the water channel alongside the road and another in a ditch, a pair of brown shoes and the match of the black shoe. On the Belfast Road he spotted a bicycle lying in a field, just on the far side of the hedge.

The abandoned bike had also been spotted by farm labourer Bob McCullough, who was putting on new gates at a field near the Upper Damolly crossroads. He and Charles passed comment on the finds before bidding farewell. About 9.30am, McCullough left what he was doing and went off to collect a sledge hammer. What he found instead, however, filled him with dread. Scattered across the fields were items of women's clothing, some of it bloodstained.

Nearby was the home of Margaret Gamble and it was to there that McCullough went for help. His arrival on her doorstep, and the news he had to tell, must have chilled Mrs Gamble to the bone. Her 19-year-old daughter, Pearl, still hadn't returned home from a dance the previous evening and she was beside herself with worry.

Grabbing hold of her young daughter Eleanor, she went with McCullough to the crossroads. There she found Pearl's handbag, brush, comb, coat, belt, skirt and pants. Painfully she gathered the items up and carried them home while McCullough phoned the police. Shortly after 5pm that evening, at a place known as Weir's Rocks, Pearl's body was found. She was naked, apart from her badly torn stockings, and her body had been thrown face down into bushes. Her woollen sweater, white blouse, white underskirt and bra had been thrown on top of her.

Less than an hour before the body was found, Robert Andrew McGladdery, one of a number of young men interviewed by police about Pearl's disappearance, was being quizzed in Newry RUC station. He and the girl had been friends since childhood and had danced together the previous evening. McGladdery fumed to detectives: "I wish I could get my hands on the boy that done this, you wouldn't have to deal with him." By

Newry shop assistant Pearl Gamble, whose
battered and near naked body was found dumped
in bushes close to her home.

the time the 24-year-old had left the station, however, the police officers on the case already suspected they had questioned the man responsible. Proving it, however, was another matter altogether.

The first task, of course, was to piece together as best they could what had happened in the previous 24 hours. Pearl, who worked as a shop assistant in Newry, had left for the dance in the Henry Thompson Memorial Orange Hall in the town with two friends, Rae Boyd and namesake, but no relation, Evelyn Gamble. They arrived there at about 10.30pm.

'Robbie' McGladdery, accompanied by a friend, William Copeland, was not to reach the hall until almost an hour later. The young men had spent most of the day together drinking after meeting in Hollywood's pub in Hill Street. They met back there in the early evening, moving on to Magee's public house on Merchant's Quay a short time later. After brief stops at the nearby St Catherine's Club, and the Royal British Legion Club in Monaghan Street, they arrived at the Orange Hall already the worse for wear.

Towards the end of the evening, McGladdery and Pearl danced together at least twice, but if he had romance in mind things obviously weren't working out. At his subsequent trial, one witness said McGladdery "was trying to hold Pearl tightly towards him and had his head bent down towards her face. But Pearl kept turning away from him".

McGladdery, dressed in a light blue suit, then asked the band to play a popular song of the day, "It's Now or Never," during which he stood by the doorway "wringing his hands". He left the hall shortly afterwards, not waiting for the 2am finish of the dance. Pearl, meanwhile, had finished the evening with another boy. After saying goodnight to him outside, she and her two girlfriends accepted a lift, with Pearl being dropped at the Upper Damolly crossroads, close to her home. It was the last time she was seen alive by anyone but her killer.

From the injuries she sustained and the evidence at hand, it was obvious Pearl had been attacked within seconds of alighting from the car. She had been struck about the face and dragged through a gap in the hedges. Pearl, however, had put up a brave struggle from the outset and evidently continued to resist for as long as she could. Approximately 130 yards into the field, the grass was bloodied where McGladdery had tried to beat the resistence out of her. Further along, her clothes ripped from her body and possibly semiconscious, the murderer completed his brutality. A postmortem revealed an horrendous list of injuries, including a broken nose, severe bruising around the eyes and left cheek, and cuts around her lips. But these were superficial compared to the star-shaped "puncture" wounds, most about two inches deep, inflicted about the body, including near the right ear and forehead, but particularly to the chest. One had punctured the heart and would have led to death, had not McGladdery finished the job by strangulation. Despite the sexual nature of the attack, she had not been raped.

McGladdery, who had raced his victim to the murder scene on a bike stolen from outside the Orange Hall, now made his way home to dispose of his blood-stained clothes. Early next morning he was up and about unusually early, and was seen bringing water into the house. This he evidently used to throughly clean himself in a bid to remove any tell-tale evidence. Later that Saturday evening, after being quizzed by the RUC in Newry, he was examined by a police doctor, who took forensic samples. The medic noted how exceptionally clean McGladdery was and that his skin was a reddish colour as if it had been scrubbed almost raw.

No amount of scrubbing, however, could remove the scratch marks from his skin, which no one could recall having seen the previous evening. Asked how they were inflicted, McGladdery told police a chest expander had slipped, striking him in the face. He wasn't believed, of course, and his home was searched. This yielded a book, Micky Spillane's "The Long Wait," which bore star-shaped marks similar to the wounds inflicted on Pearl. These had been caused, it was believed, by the tang (the bit which fits into a wooden handle) of a file. McGladdery, it was known, had bought two files on the Friday for use in a small shoe repairing business he operated from home.

Vital pieces of the evidence jigsaw were still missing, however, including McGladdery's blood-stained clothes and the murder weapon. Convinced they knew their man, the police began to harass McGladdery, constantly watching him and subjecting him to regular questioning. Sooner or later, they knew, he would make a mistake.

On 9th February, 1961, McGladdery was spotted by Constable Donald Keown leaving Fallone's cafe in Hill Street and making his way to the Savoy Cinema. The officer waited for him to re-emerge, which he did about 11.20pm, returning to the cafe. Shortly before midnight, McGladdery was again on the move, pausing briefly to talk to someone in Hill Street. Suddenly, without warning, he sprinted away, losing the pursuing constable along the Downshire Road. Const Keown made his way to McGladdery's house, but he wasn't there. At 12.45am, he arrived home via Damolly Lane.

At daybreak the police moved in to search the area, convinced that McGladdery had been either disposing of evidence or checking that his earlier cover-up was secure. In a field, a little more than 300 yards from McGladdery's house, they discovered an old septic tank. Using a stick to probe the bottom, officers hooked a bag, weighted down by a large stone, from the stinking waters. Inside was an overcoat, vest and hankerchief, all bearing what appeared to be bloodstains. There was also a neck-tie, believed to have been the murder weapon. McGladdery was promptly arrested.

Pearl's murder had caused outrage across the Province and, naturally, nowhere more so than in Newry. When McGladdery appeared at the town's courthouse in April it was beseiged by a 500-strong crowd, the vast majority of whom were excluded from the courtroom for sheer want of space. Inside there was high drama, with McGladdery's mother, Agnes, attempting to clasp her son's hand as he sat in the dock, only to be restrained by two warders and a policeman. A bid was made to have the trial heard in County Fermanagh because of alleged prejudice and the publication of Press articles considered to be in contempt of court.

In the event, the trial was held at Downpatrick in October before Lord Justice Curran. In his opening address, Brian Maginness, the Attorney-General, told the court:

Robbie McGladdery, the last man to be hanged in Northern Ireland, led the police a merry dance before the evidence could be found to arrest him.

> *The sum total of this evidence points in one direction only - that McGladdery on that early morning of January 28, foully and deliberately murdered this young girl. The taking off of her clothes suggests a sexual motive, and although it is not necessary for the Crown to prove motive, you may come to the conclusion that passion started this affair. And an unrequited passion may have been succeeded by hate or anger.*

After five days of evidence, the all-male jury took just 40 minutes to bring in their verdict of guilty. The execution date was set for 7th November, but was delayed after McGladdery unsuccessfully appealed. At 8am, on Wednesday, 20th December, 1961, just five days before Christmas, McGladdery became the last man to be hanged in Northern Ireland. Approximately 30 people gathered outside the jail on the day of execution. One assumes many more would have made the effort if they had known its significance. At 8.05am, when a notice declaring that the sentence of death had been carried out was posted on the wicket gate, they moved forward to read it before dispersing. Inside the jail, an inquest held shortly after the execution returned a verdict of death due to the fracture of the cervical spine after judicial hanging. As the soil was returned to McGladdery's unmarked grave within the prison walls, it brought to an end a controversial chapter in the prison's history which is unlikely ever to be reopened.

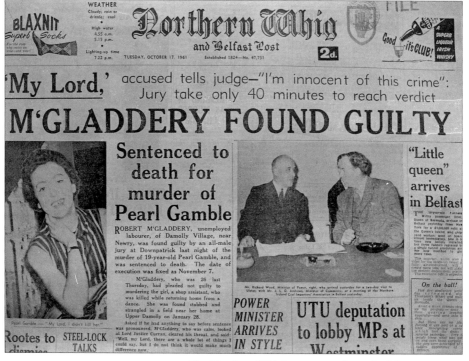

The Northern Whig's report on the end of the court case.

CHAPTER FOURTEEN

IN CONCLUSION

*It did stick with me. It was traumatic at
the time. It must have been, I suppose,
three or four months before I got over it.*

A former death-watch warder

Northern Ireland Prime Minister
Captain Terence O'Neill, left, with Taoiseach
Jack Lynch and Brian Faulkner, who later became
one of the last Stormont premiers (News Letter).

CONCERNS over capital punishment in the last 150 years of its existence resulted in investigations by two Royal Commissions and two Select Committees. The first of these sat in 1819, the last from 1949 to 1953. While some raised the odd doubt, they generally endorsed hanging as the best method of dealing with murderers.

Arguments on the issue raged elsewhere, of course, but nowhere more fiercely than in Northern Ireland in the wake of the two executions of 1961. The Stormont government came under tremendous pressure to change the law. A series of Parliamentary debates showed the Unionist Party was split on the issue, with the Opposition almost exclusively anti-noose. Privately, the Cabinet agreed that some reform of the law was necessary, but was reluctant to go public for fear of inflaming both the pro and anti-hanging lobbies any further.

In November, 1963, however, the problem came to a head when Stormont's only Liberal MP, Sheelagh Murnaghan, brought forward a Private Member's Bill, the Homicide and Criminal Responsibility Bill, which included the abolition of capital punishment. Guaranteed the support of Opposition members, the Cabinet feared enough Unionists would also give their backing for it to be passed, and so let it be known they were prepared to bring forward their own proposals. The Murnaghan Bill was subsequently defeated, but only by four votes.

The following year, the Northern Ireland Government, led by Prime Minister Captain Terence O'Neill, reaffirmed its commitment to bring foward legislation for the abolition of hanging. At the same time, capital punishment was suspended in Great Britain for an experimental five year period. The tide had finally turned in favour of those opposed to State executions.

When the Criminal Justice Act, published in 1965 but not passed until the following year, finally came before Stormont, however, it was not as total as many had wanted. Citing four types of murder still punishable by death, it led to a Unionist revolt which ensured some concessions. Even so, in its final form the Bill abolished hanging for "normal" murder, but still applied the ultimate penalty to two categories: the killing of a police officer or Crown servant, or any person assisting them in the execution of their duty, such as prison warders; and killings "in the course or furtherance of any seditious act or conspiracy to further the activites or aims of seditious organisations". In other words, terrorist-related murders. If such a law had existed since the creation of the Northern Ireland state, only one man, IRA killer Tom Williams, would have been executed under it.

Despite its shortcomings, the 1966 Act actually put Northern Ireland ahead of Great Britain, which wasn't to abolish hanging permanently until 1969. It, too, retained exclusion clauses allowing for the execution of those found guilty of treason, arson in Her Majesty's dockyard and piracy on the high seas, with a gallows being retained at Wandsworth Prison.

At Belfast Prison, the scaffold was also intact and was to remain so for a number of years yet. Although Westminster was unhappy at the anomoly between Great Britain and Northern Ireland, and said so privately, it was to wait another four years before it could do something about it.

With the violence of the late Sixties and early Seventies, it was only a matter of time before a sentence of death was to be again passed in Northern Ireland. That day arrived in February, 1973, when Albert Edward Browne, a member of the then legal Ulster Defence Association, was convicted of murdering a policeman in October of the previous year and condemned to be hanged. Mr Justice McGonigal, who passed sentence on 29-year-old Browne at the Belfast City Commission, did not don the

Lord Willie Whitelaw, a former Secretary of State for Northern Ireland, incorporated into the Emergency Provisions Bill the legislation bringing the Province's laws on capital punishment into line with those operating in Great Britain (News Letter).

traditional black cap. The execution date was set for 25th April but, on the 6th April, Secretary of State William Whitelaw used his powers under Section One of the Northern Ireland (Temporary Provisions) Act to commute the sentence to life imprisonment. Browne was told of the decision in the condemned cell at Crumlin Road Jail.

Later that month, a 19-year-old Roman Catholic, William Gerard Holden, was sentenced to death for the murder of a soldier. He also took up residence in the condemned cell, but had not long to wait. A clause inserted in the Northern Ireland Emergency Provisions Bill, bringing the Province's capital punishment laws into line with those applying in Great Britain, came before MPs at Westminister on 15th May, and was overwhelmingly passed. A few hours later, Holden, the last man to be condemned to die by an Ulster court, was told his sentence had been commuted to imprisonment for life.

The scaffold at the end of C-wing in Belfast Prison could, at long last, be dismantled. The jail burying ground, alongside the garden wall, had received its last victim.

The political debate over capital punishment, and its possible restoration, has not gone away, however. Barely two years after abolition in Great Britain, a bid was made to bring back hanging. Since then there have been similar votes in the Commons on a regular basis, including 1972, twice in 1973, 1974, 1975, 1979, 1982, 1983, 1987, 1988, 1990 and most recently at time of writing, February 1994. As the years have went on, the Parliamentary majority opposed to restoration has grown, while public opinion polls have tended to show the opposite trend, with a fluctuating but generally growing demand for the return of the noose, particularly for terrorist offences.

Crumlin Road Jail is itself now under sentence of death. As it marks the 150th anniversary of its completion, the cost of modernising its facilities makes its retention more expensive than building a replacement. Assuming the paramilitary ceasefires continue, there will also be less need to maintain the present level of prison accommodation in Northern Ireland which 25 years of violence demanded. In short, a reprieve for Her Majesty's Prison, Belfast, appears unlikely and it seems only an execution date remains to be set.

The last word, however, should go to a man who had more experience of capital punishment, literally at first hand, than anyone. Executioner Albert Pierrepoint wrote in his 1974 autobiography:

> *The fruit of my experience has this bitter aftertaste; that I do not now believe that any one of the hundreds of executions I carried out has in any way acted as a deterrent against future murder. Capital punishment in my view, achieved nothing except revenge.*

SOURCES

BOOKS:

Hangmen of England: A History of Execution from Jack Ketch to Albert Pierrepoint,
 by Brian Bailey
The Fatal Gallows Tree, by John Deane Potter
Lords of the Scaffold: A History of Execution, by Geoffrey Abbot
My Experiences as an Executioner, by James Berry
Executioner: Pierrepoint, by Albert Pierrepoint
The Humanitarian Theory of Punishment and Babbage, by C S Lewis
The History of Capital Punishment, by George Ryley Scott
Reflections on Hanging, by Arthur Koestler
Hanged By The Neck, by Arthur Koestler
The Hangmen of England, by Horace Bleackley
When the State Kills, Amnesty International
A New Handbook on Hanging, by Charles Duff
History of Ireland, 1603-1923, by J C Beckett
The Making of Modern Ireland, by J C Beckett
The Green Flag, by Robert Kee
The Irish Sketch Book, 1842, by William Makepeace Thackeray
The Life and Times of Mary Ann McCracken: A Belfast Panorama, by Mary McNeill
Belfast: An Illustrated Architectural Guide, by Paul Larmour
Buildings of Belfast, 1700-1914, by C E B Brett.
Belfast: An Illustrated History, by Jonathan Bardon
A Belfast Chronicle, 1789: A compilation from the Belfast News Letter,
 by James McAllister
Belfast: the Making of the City, by J C Beckett et al
No Mean City: Belfast 1880-1914, by Brian Walker and Hugh Dixon
Central Belfast: A Historical Gazetteer, by Marcus Patton
Faces of the Past, by Brian Mercer Walker
Famous Irish Lives, by Martin Wallace
Walks Among the Poor of Belfast, by the Rev W M O'Hanlon
Anglo-Norman Ulster: The History and Archaeology of an Irish Barony, 1177-1400,
 by T E McNeill
Historical Notices of Old Belfast and its Vicinity, Robert M Young
Revolt in the North: Antrim and Down in 1798, by Charles Dickson
Ulster in '98: Episodes and Anecdotes, by Robert M Young
Antrim and Down in '98, by Dr Richard Robert Madden
The Unfortunate Mr Robert Emmet, by Leon O'Broin
Irish Battles: A Military History of Ireland, by G A Hayes-McCoy

Roger Casement, by Rene MacColl

The Royal Irish Constabulary: An Oral History, by John Brewer

Arresting Memories, by R J K Sinclair and F J M Scully

The Secret Army: A History of the IRA 1916-70, by J Bowyer Bell

The IRA, by Tim Pat Coogan

Gravestone Inscriptions, various volumes

The Operational Policy in Belfast Prison for the Management of Paramilitary Prisoners from Opposing Factions, by The Viscount Colville of Culross QC

NEWSPAPERS:

Belfast News Letter, Belfast Telegraph, Irish News, Northern Whig, Banner of Ulster, Belfast Morning News, The Belfast Mercury, Belfast Commercial Chronicle, Armagh Guardian, Newry Telegraph, Newry Reporter, Coleraine Chronicle.